SIDE by SIDE

SIDE SIDE

SUPPORTING A SPOUSE IN CHURCH SERVICE

JEANETTE GOATES SMITH, L.M.F.T.

DESERET
BOOK

SALT LAKE CITY, UTAH

For Bret
who is my hero

Visit us at deseretbook.com

Library of Congress Cataloging-in-Publication Data

Smith, JeaNette Goates.
    Side by side : supporting a spouse in church service / JeaNette Goates Smith.
        p.   cm.
    Includes index.
    ISBN 1-57008-894-2 (pbk.)
    1. Spouses—Religious life. 2. Married people in church work. 3. Church work—Church of Jesus Christ of Latter-day Saints. I. Title.

    BX8641.S635 2004
    253'.22—dc21   2003001835

Printed in the United States of America   72076
Publishers Printing, Salt Lake City, UT

10   9   8   7   6   5   4   3   2   1

CONTENTS

PART THREE: TAKING CARE OF THE CHILDREN

PART FOUR: TAKING CARE OF THE FLOCK

INTRODUCTION

"CONGRATULATIONS!" YOUR SWEETHEART HAS JUST been called to serve in a very responsible position in The Church of Jesus Christ of Latter-day Saints. Oops. Perhaps congratulations are not in order. Some might think "Condolences" would be the better sentiment. You two could become strangers passing in the night with this new assignment. While it's true your spouse—and your family—will have many wonderful, uplifting experiences upon accepting a call to serve, and his or her worthiness and willingness to serve certainly warrants hearty congratulations, a demanding tenure of service presents new challenges for your marital relationship. What's the appropriate sentiment upon receiving a call to serve?

With careful planning, the experience of supporting your spouse in a Church calling can strengthen rather than weaken your marriage. You can enjoy all the blessings that come from being married to a worthy, capable servant of the Lord, and at the same time assure Church service does nothing to your marriage except make it richer.

The purpose of this book is to help you find the joy inherent in serving the Lord, while simultaneously realizing greater joy in your marriage. The two goals are not incompatible. In fact, they complement one another. Couples need not become strangers during a period of demanding Church service. You can actually find *greater* joy in your marriage when your spouse is steeped in Church service than you did when his or her time was more available to you.

The book is divided into four parts: caring for your spouse, caring for yourself, caring for the children, and caring for the flock. You might be tempted to jump right into the middle of the book and immediately begin lightening your own load. You may truly desire a survival guide to help you endure your spouse's tenure of service. Forget supporting your spouse, how can the wife of a devoted Church leader face all the challenges that come her way? Please have faith, read the chapters about supporting your spouse. As you discover the absolutely vital role you play in your loved one's ability to serve, your perspective about your role will change, and this is the first step to lifting your own load.

At least two types of stress enter into the lives of busy Church servants: emotional and physical. These same types of stress affect the spouses of busy Church servants. In this book you will learn to help your spouse alleviate these different types of stress that may accompany a calling. Plus, you will learn to alleviate your own stress.

The first quarter of the book will help you learn how to be a support to your spouse. You'll learn how to

- share his (or her) burden
- lighten that burden

- identify people you would never have dreamed could become a resource to you
- understand the true nature of support (what we traditionally think of as supporting a spouse may actually *add* to both of your burdens)
- become an effective sounding board
- counsel wisely
- cheer your spouse on
- honor confidential information

The heart of the book will help you make sure *your own* emotional and physical needs are met when your spouse is involved in Church service, including how to

- minimize the amount of time your spouse spends away from home
- safeguard the unity of your relationship in the midst of competing priorities
- combat loneliness when your spouse spends time away from you
- protect yourself from feeling resentful

The next section will help you attend to the needs of the children. You will discover ways to

- deal with public scrutiny
- ensure your children do not resent being set up as examples
- ensure your children do not come to resent their Church-leader parent's frequent absences

The remainder of the book will conclude with suggestions for keeping your flock happy, emotionally and physically. You can bless the members of your organization most effectively when you

- purify your motives for service
- care as deeply as your spouse cares about the flock
- perform acts of service that invigorate rather than drain you as a couple
- avoid discouragement when those you serve do not progress

In the following chapters I will share what I have learned from years of counseling Latter-day Saints who, along with their spouses, lose themselves in Church service. I also draw from experiences as the daughter of a Saint devoted to Church service and the wife of a Saint who is equally vested in such service. In addition, serving in eleven different wards across the United States—from the West to the Midwest to the Northeast to the South—has given me a diverse perspective of members and callings in the Church. (If you read any stories that sound familiar, remember they could have occurred anywhere in the world, at any time in the past forty years. And yes, you guessed correctly, I have changed some of the names and the details to honor people's privacy.)

On every page of this book is my prayer for you that you will not be weary in well-doing. We are "laying the foundation of a great work" (D&C 64:33). Ours is the work of the Lord, and this great work will roll forth. We are invited for a brief moment in history to accomplish deeds that will affect the eternities but not for one minute compromise the unity of our individual families.

PART ONE

TAKING CARE OF
YOUR SPOUSE

CHAPTER 1

SERVICE: IT'S WHAT WE DO

WHEN I WAS A LITTLE GIRL, I USED TO DREAM ABOUT the type of person I wanted to marry. I dreamed about marrying someone who was an active member of the Church, who loved the Savior, and who wanted to devote his life to service. With an active Latter-day Saint spouse I could be sure my family would kneel together each morning and evening to hold a family prayer. My dreams included fun family home evenings where children would enthusiastically raise their hands to participate. Together my sweetheart and I would attend church, the whole family lined up on a pew, with Mom and Dad sitting together holding hands. My goal to marry an active member of the Church would assure that such dreams would come true.

Years after pondering the qualities I wanted in a spouse, my dreams came true. My sweetheart is the personification of an active Latter-day Saint—"believing, behaving, and serving," to use the words of Elder Neal A. Maxwell (in "News of the Church," *Ensign,* September 1983, 75). I am experiencing all the blessings I dreamed of as a youth. However, along with all those blessings I envisioned long ago came responsibility—responsibility I never could have imagined.

Perhaps you have had the same experience. As a covenant-keeping Latter-day Saint, your active spouse spends extraordinary amounts of time and energy serving the Lord. You probably never dreamed that the time and effort your spouse puts into serving the Lord could become so overwhelming. Perhaps you're immersed in a week that looks like this:

Monday—family home evening
Tuesday—Boy Scout merit badge workshop
Wednesday—Young Women's program
Thursday—stake meetings
Friday—baptism
Saturday—youth dance
Sunday—you know all about Sundays!

And your spouse can't even sit with you all-lined-up-as-a-family-on-the-pew on Sundays, because your sweetheart has to visit other wards and stakes or sit on the stand! During these periods of enormous responsibility we might question those dreams of our youth. At times like these we might wonder what exactly we were thinking when we put "active LDS" at the top of the list describing a future spouse. At times we may even wish our spouses weren't quite so "active." But of course we don't mean it.

TO BE OR NOT TO BE

Can anyone be an active Latter-day Saint and refuse to serve in the Lord's kingdom? Is it possible for us to claim the tremendous blessings of the gospel without the tremendous responsibility?

I once had a conversation with a vegetarian who forced a parallel question. I sat next to her at a dinner party, and we started discussing the merits of being a vegetarian. I revealed to the woman that I would prefer eating like a vegetarian myself but it's too inconvenient to eat that way 100 percent of the time. So even though I like the idea of eating like a vegetarian, I'm not willing to put forth the effort.

"I guess you could call me an 'inactive vegetarian,'" I chuckled.

She didn't appreciate my joke in the least. She looked at me as though I had broccoli growing from my ears. "Either you're a vegetarian or you're not," she replied, highly offended. "There's no such thing as an 'inactive' vegetarian."

She sure taught me a lesson. Vegetarians, by definition, do not eat meat. If you eat meat you're not a vegetarian. It's pretty simple. You're either a vegetarian or you aren't.

The conversation reminded me of our commitment as Latter-day Saints. We make covenants at baptism to take upon us the name of Christ, to serve him to the end (see D&C 20:37). By definition, Latter-day Saints serve. At times your Church service will be more demanding than at others, but in one capacity or another, a covenant-keeping Latter-day Saint serves.

One Church writer expressed it this way: "Exaltation depends on how much you are willing to give. It begins with the offering of a broken heart and a contrite spirit upon the altar of the Lord, and it grows as we dedicate ourselves through covenants to serving our fellowmen, our spouses, and our posterity. To become as God is, we must learn to give freely, to love freely, to be willing to suffer even the humiliation and sorrow of seeing our love rejected— willing to love all as God loves us, unconditionally, throughout eternity" (Gordon C. Thomasson, "Becoming Saviors on Mount

5

Zion: The Place of Suffering in the Gospel of Unselfishness," *New Era,* April 1973, 13).

Even though we know service is an inherent part of being an active Latter-day Saint, it's not uncommon for the spouse of a deeply involved Church servant to have to make some adjustments in her outlook and priorities.

Once I congratulated a new Young Men president on his calling. He responded with some good humor. "Yeah, I guess I should have told the bishop about my Word of Wisdom problem," he laughed.

"Do you think you can get off the hook that easily?" I joked back.

Humor is known to reveal our innermost feelings. Such humor about Church callings tells us Church service can be the cause of serious fear and trepidation.

Service to the Lord can, at times, seem overwhelming and can take its toll on a couple. When you are awakened at one in the morning for the third night in a week with yet another crisis, you can't help but feel some stress, perhaps even irritation.

But during the day, when you're thinking clearly and your wits are about you, you realize that although being married to a covenant-keeping servant of the Lord may seem overwhelming at times, you wouldn't want it any other way.

As discouraging and overwhelming and lonely as service to the Lord can become, ceasing your service to the Lord simply isn't an option. The only real option is to learn to see things in a whole new way, a more positive, mature way, so that the demands don't cause undue stress on your marriage and your family life.

THE GREATEST AMONG US

When I was a little girl my father served as the bishop of our ward in Albuquerque, New Mexico. Back then I thought that callings in the Church were about glamour and prestige. I remember feeling so honored when Dad stood at the podium to conduct a meeting. I sat up a little straighter in the pew when someone bore testimony about how much Bishop Goates had blessed the person's life. Once a week Dad conducted interviews at home. Young men and young women from the ward filled our living room while waiting their turn for an interview in Dad's study. We entertained them, and they entertained us. We were filled with delight, as our home became a hub of Church activity.

Saturdays felt like paradise as Dad took us to the apple orchard that was our ward's welfare responsibility. Nothing could be more fun than "playing" with Dad in the apple orchard, as he and the rest of our ward members climbed trees and picked apples during the fall harvest. Each week we held a contest to see who could find the biggest apple in the orchard. We also marveled at the person who discovered an apple the size of a quarter. How clever our Dad was as he invented new ways to pick the apples from the tree without climbing a ladder. We thought having our dad serve as the bishop was about the neatest thing that could happen to a family.

THE LEAST AMONG US

Thirty years later my husband was called to serve as a bishop, and I learned a lot about serving the Lord that I didn't understand at age eight. I learned that service is not at all about glamour and prestige. Service to the Lord is about humility, love, and hard work. I learned that "he who is the greatest among you shall be the servant of all." I learned that the glamour and prestige of the world don't hold a candle to the warmth and comfort of the Spirit telling you in your heart the Lord is well-pleased.

The Savior taught us the meaning of leadership through a poignant example. He washed his disciples' feet. Imagine the Savior performing such an act. Imagine the Creator of the earth and seas and skies—the Savior of mankind, the Son of God, who could command the elements and they would obey—sitting in the dirt, with a mud-caked foot in his lap, rubbing his hands across dry, cracking heels, scrubbing between dirty toes, and underneath toenails. Leadership doesn't look all that glamorous when seen in this light.

When my husband served as the bishop we had a sister in our ward who was married to a man twenty years her senior. She was in her seventies, and her husband had lived almost a full century. This sister watched over her husband in a tender and caring way. He was incontinent, so she helped him to the bathroom every few hours. When her timing failed, she cleaned up his accidents. He had a serious fungus upon which this sister rubbed medicine several times a day.

One weekend this sister wanted to go out of town to attend her granddaughter's wedding. However, she could not leave unless someone watched her husband, so my husband and I volunteered. Every two hours throughout the night my husband rose and helped the elderly brother to the bathroom. My dear husband rubbed medicine on the terrible, painful fungus this brother fought. My dear husband listened to this brother moan, and ached to see his pain.

Their voices echoed from the bathroom throughout that night. And as I heard the man moaning, "Oh, Bishop, oh, Bishop," to the front of my mind crept the image of Jesus washing feet. And I loved both the Savior and my husband more deeply than I had ever loved.

THE MAKING OR THE BREAKING

The kind of demanding service that may be required of a Latter-day Saint couple can be dealt with like any other trial in a marriage—a stressful career, a passel of active children, a major move, or having to care for aging parents. A couple can grow closer through the trial, or they can grow more distant. Ideally, Church service will strengthen our marriages rather than strain them.

Working together in the service of our Heavenly Father can strengthen all kinds of relationships. Missionaries may make life-long friends with companions they serve with in the mission field. Serving in a presidency together can spark a friendship that lasts far beyond the service. A couple who serve the Lord together can also grow together and their relationship blossom in ways it never would without their serving together.

By contrast, serving together doesn't guarantee the servants will strengthen their interpersonal relationships. Sometimes missionaries don't get along with their companions and they request transfers. Some presidencies do not experience unity and they request a release. Likewise, some marriages find that one spouse's Church service can strain the marriage.

The Lord does not give us commandments for the purpose of bringing unhappiness. Every commandment he gives is intended to bring us joy: "He doeth not anything save it be for the benefit of the world; for he loveth the world, even that he layeth down his own life that he may draw all men unto him. Wherefore, he commandeth none that they shall not partake of his salvation" (2 Nephi 26:24).

9

Some individuals may think that service is only about blessing others' lives. In reality, our own lives are blessed as much or more than the lives of those we serve. Our Heavenly Father does not command us to serve others to our own detriment. Service in the kingdom is intended to bless both the recipient of the service and the giver of the service.

Service in the kingdom is not intended to strain the marital relationship of the servants. Service in the kingdom is a means to strengthen a marriage. I am absolutely certain that one of the hidden blessings of supporting a spouse in his or her Church service is a vastly improved marriage. The Lord pours out blessings upon couples who serve him. He pours out blessings in such abundance that we can barely contain them.

Remember the adage "Whatever doesn't kill you will make you stronger." Church service that is demanding, like any trial, can damage your marital relationship, or it can strengthen the relationship. It all depends on you. Ideally, service to the Lord can improve the quality of your marital relationship. As you and your spouse serve the Lord together, the love between you can grow stronger, you can feel more appreciative of one another, and you can feel one in purpose and become more unified.

The possibility of such great blessings makes Church service an ideal opportunity to improve your marital relationship, not stress it. Achieving a celestial marriage is a requirement every bit as important to achieving exaltation as service in the kingdom. Concerning celestial marriage, Elder Hugh B. Brown of the Quorum of the Twelve Apostles wrote: "When one accepts the conditions and obligations of this eternal partnership, he must realize that failure here is almost total failure. Whatever his successes may be in other fields of activity, if a man fails to discharge the obligations imposed by the eternal covenant, the appalling penalty will be the loss of celestial glory, accompanied by responsibility for the losses sustained by those with whom he made the contract and for whom he is responsible" ("The LDS Concept of Marriage," *Ensign,* January 1972, 63).

No one can afford to let Church service damage his or her marriage. Neither should we "opt out" and refuse to serve. Our eternal salvation depends on both the quality of our service and the quality of our marriages. There is no choosing one commitment over the other. A covenant-keeping Latter-day Saint serves in the kingdom and at the same time creates a celestial marriage. In fact, by asking you to serve in his kingdom the Lord is giving you a perfect opportunity to create the kind of marriage that could be described as celestial. Let service strengthen your relationships, not damage them. The stakes are too high to consider ignoring either obligation.

REALITY STRIKES

How can you, when you are married to someone who gives and gives and gives to others, to the point where you may feel neglected (and wonder if perhaps you have been forgotten entirely)—how can you retain the fire in your heart, the desire to serve, the desire to support your spouse? How can you retain the joy that can be found in watching and helping your spouse go about the work of the Lord?

Can you maintain your enthusiasm for serving the Lord when your computer is down, and has been for months, and your spouse is too busy to fix it?

Can you welcome your spouse delightedly into your arms when you have eaten dinner alone and the homemade rolls you baked are cold on the counter, and your spouse announces there is a stake dance this weekend that you two will need to chaperone and that's where you'll spend your date night?

Can you keep the cheerful singsong in your voice when the telephone rings, just after you have fallen asleep, and it's for your spouse, and it's the same person who woke you up the previous night?

Absolutely and unequivocally, yes! This is the Lord's work, and it is the most important work in the world. The Lord will not ask us to run faster than we are able (see Mosiah 4:27), and he won't ask us to do anything we are not capable of doing (see 1 Nephi 3:7). If he asks us to serve in demanding capacities, he will strengthen our backs and help us find a way to do it.

Of course there is a way to engage in this wonderful work to which you are committed, this work which you know to be true, without jeopardizing your family relationships. This is a work that will bring joy eternally and immediately. You can even do it without becoming utterly exhausted, discouraged, and overwhelmed.

THE ETERNAL "TO DO" LIST

A valiant Church servant may be tempted to become a workaholic, constantly working on his or her Church calling. If you have served in the Church for very long, you know one thing: the work is never done. After all, there are only eleven million Latter-day Saints in the world, and there are six billion people. That's a lot of people to share the gospel with. In addition, of those eleven million Latter-day Saints, you will notice that less than half attend meetings regularly. You don't have to look very far to find someone who needs your help. There is always someone new to reactivate, to fellowship, or to share the gospel with.

If you're the type of person who feels peace only after crossing every item off your "to do" list, you will not feel peace serving in the kingdom. Saying, "I'm going to finish my Church work once and for all" is like saying, "I'm going to eat once and for all." Bringing our fellowmen to a higher plane of living is a job that is never done.

Young mothers know exactly how it feels to have a perpetual "to do" list. As soon as you cook a meal, the family is hungry again. Just when the house appears spotless, the children run inside and it becomes dirty again. (That's why, as a young mother, I always enjoyed sewing. At some point in time the dress is finished, and it doesn't need to be sewn all over again as soon as someone wears it.)

A young mother eventually learns that floors will always be there to scrub, but her children won't always be there to nurture. She takes the time to build relationships with her children so when they leave the home they will still enjoy close family ties.

The same principle holds true in a family where one of the parents is heavily involved in Church service. There is always more work to do in the Lord's kingdom. We must decide how much of that work we can take on ourselves and still fulfill our callings as husbands, wives, mothers, and fathers. Church service is part of our covenant relationship with our Heavenly Father, but so is parenting and so is developing an eternal marriage. Balancing all three is part of a great learning process.

Husbands and wives cannot put the family ties on hold for a few years while they serve in a demanding Church calling and expect to pick up again where they left off once the tenure of service is over. Couples will want to remain close to the family throughout a lifetime of Church service.

THE ETERNAL FAMILY

"You will be a bishop for only a few years [or an elders quorum president or a Scoutmaster], but you'll always be a dad, and you'll always be a husband." So said President Ezra Taft Benson in his talk entitled "To the Fathers in Israel," adding, "Remember your sacred calling as a father in Israel—your most important calling in time and eternity—a calling from which you will never be released" (*Ensign,* November 1987, 51). Likewise, a sister will serve as a Relief Society president or a Primary president or a Young Women president for only a few years, but she will always be a mom, and she will always be a wife.

Let us never forget the purposes of our Heavenly Father. Heavenly Father wants us to have joy. "Men are, that they might have joy" (2 Nephi 2:25). Naturally, if Heavenly Father wants us to have joy, everything he tells us to do will help us achieve that purpose: realize joy. Every commandment given by our Heavenly Father is to help us find joy. When he asks us to serve in the kingdom, he intends for us to find joy in that service. If service to our Heavenly Father is not fulfilling, something's missing—we're not doing it as the Lord intended. Therefore, if our service damages relationships with precious family members, we're not serving as the Lord intended.

I've always thought it extremely kind of our Heavenly Father to command us to put our families first among our priorities. Not only does he tell us to put our families first among our priorities but he also tells us to put our spouse first among our family members. Like all of Father's commandments, this commandment is designed to bring us joy. He commands us to nurture our marital relationships and those relationships with our family members—the very relationships that can bring us the most joy on this earth. How blessed we are that the very priority that will bring us the most joy is the priority Heavenly Father wants us to select. It's like begging us to open a box of chocolates and choose our very favorite one—well, if you insist, I think I can manage.

CHAPTER 2

⌒

THE NECESSARY
SPOUSE

NOT LONG AGO I ATTENDED THE FUNERAL OF
President Harold B. Lee's daughter, Helen Lee Goates. Helen's
former bishop, David Checketts, spoke. Bishop Checketts had
been a missionary in the California Arcadia Mission when Helen
served with her husband, Brent, as Elder Checketts's mission president. Coincidentally, twenty years after serving as a missionary
in Elder Goates's mission, Elder Checketts served as President
Goates's bishop.

Bishop Checketts described what it was like to be a missionary
serving with President and Sister Goates. He admired President
Goates, and watched him carefully to learn leadership skills. As an
assistant to the president, he noticed the breakneck pace President
Goates kept. He also saw what a heavy load the president bore.
Often Elder Checketts wondered how President Goates could
shoulder such a huge responsibility. "He holds all of us up," Elder
Checketts mused to himself. "Who holds him up?"

One evening after a long weekend of zone conferences, Elder

Checketts was driving President and Sister Goates back to the mission home. Together the mission president and his wife snuggled in the back seat of the Buick Regal. "You did a wonderful job today, Elder Goates," Helen said admiringly to her husband. "You are truly an inspiration to these young missionaries." She looked into her husband's eyes and laid her head on his shoulder. Elder Goates placed his arm around her shoulders and held his sweetheart close.

Glancing in the rearview mirror, Elder Checketts thought to himself, "All is well in the California Arcadia Mission. The President has Sister Goates to hold him up."

Elder L. Tom Perry said, "Nothing can relieve the anxiety and load of being a bishop quite like the aid of a supportive companion" ("For a Bishop Must Be Blameless," *Ensign*, November 1982, 29). A spouse can literally and figuratively lighten the load of a busy servant of the Lord. Regardless of the leadership position your spouse holds, he or she will serve more effectively with your loving support.

CALLED AS ONE

You get a glimpse at the importance of a spouse in a Church servant's service the very moment a calling is extended. The spouse is generally invited to be present when a calling is first extended. Together a couple discovers the nature of the calling. Together they learn the responsibility that faces the person being extended the calling. From the very moment the calling is extended, the spouse is invited to offer support. Even nonmember spouses are consulted at times, not necessarily to invite participation, but to assure that no obstacles to the member's service will come from home.

An article from the *Ensign* explains: "The Brethren have

counseled that before a wife or a child is to receive any Church calling, the ecclesiastical leaders discuss the call with the husband and receive his consent to issue the call." Likewise, "When a man is called to a position in the Church, the Brethren have counseled that the wife should be asked if she can support her husband in the new position." There is wisdom in asking about this support, as the article points out: "Callings in the Church often require a united family effort, and it is important that full support be given by all family members" (Boyd D. Beagley, "I Have a Question," *Ensign,* June 1983, 26).

We are further reminded of the importance of a spouse's support when we see that some positions cannot be filled by an individual *without* a spouse. When I was in high school we had a very popular seminary teacher named Brian Theurer, who was single. At the time, older males could teach seminary for only three years without being married. When we discovered that Brother Theurer wasn't returning to teach the next year, we went to work finding him a wife. We joked about setting him up on dates, and we prodded him to phone every unmarried woman we knew. That summer he was called to serve in a bishopric of a singles ward and by fall he had married a lovely redhead named Mejken. "It's important for the seminary students to see you as a role model," said Brother Theurer, who is now enjoying the support of his wife while serving in a calling he could not fulfill without her—bishop.

You may have heard the delightful story about how Hugh Nibley was encouraged to marry when he accepted a position at Brigham Young University. The story has been told in many forms, but his eldest daughter, Christina, tells it this way: "Daddy was hired to work at Brigham Young University when he was 36 years old, but he was not married. So he was told that he needed to marry. Obedient to the Brethren, he started looking for a wife. He never actually said he would marry the first girl he saw, as the stories go. However, he hadn't been on campus long when he met my mother. She was working in the housing office and helped him find a place to stay."

With a spouse by his side, this valiant servant of the Lord was able to contribute unparalleled scholarship to the Church.

WHY SPOUSES MATTER

Serving in a demanding calling may be likened to a man climbing a steep mountain. A high, gusty wind blowing in his face will impede his progress. On the other hand, a wind blowing against his back can aid his climb and make it seem almost effortless. A spouse's presence is like the wind. It can hinder the Church leader's ability to serve or it can enhance the Church leader's ability to serve.

President Spencer W. Kimball believed that his choice of a spouse influenced his ability to serve effectively as a member of the Quorum of the Twelve Apostles. "When you ask that one individual to be your companion," Elder Kimball told a group of missionaries, "marry her in the temple, and be sure she is better than you are. I would never be in the Council of the Twelve today if I had married some of the girls that I have known. Sister Kimball kept me growing and never let me be satisfied with mediocrity" (in Edward L. Kimball and Andrew E. Kimball Jr., *Spencer W. Kimball* [Salt Lake City: Bookcraft, 1977], 317).

Elder James E. Faust stressed the importance of a spouse, specifically a wife, in a presentation to LDS counselors and psychotherapists: "One of the areas in which our wives perform a very great service is in their loving discipline of us. In their discipline they keep us closer to what we ought to be in our holy callings. In their discipline they teach us. It is part of the polishing we need to fill in the holes in our character and smooth the rough edges and make us more adequate. Together we are a team—we are one.

"President N. Eldon Tanner's daughter Isabel says about her father, 'When Mother married Daddy, he was just a farm boy.' But she went on to say that when Sister Tanner would give him a loving suggestion, unlike many men who bridle or argue when their wives tell them something that is good for them, he would simply say, 'If you think that's what I should do, I'll do it.' Listening to Sister Tanner and listening to the Lord has made a very great man out of President Tanner" ("Brethren, Love Your Wives," in *Love* [Salt Lake City: Deseret Book, 1986], 16).

TWO HEADS BETTER THAN ONE

The Lord's plan for mankind included each person finding a companion. One reason for this surely must be that companions enable us to more effectively do His work. A spouse can help a Church leader believe in himself when he suffers from self-doubt. A spouse can help a leader see the bright side of a situation when he struggles to see past the gloom. A spouse can give a leader feedback when he wants to toss an idea around. If a leader feels criticized or unappreciated a spouse reminds him that, at least to one person on earth, he means the world.

Sometimes a spouse will act like a coach, sending the leader back into the game and encouraging him to give it his all. Sometimes a spouse will act like a doctor, patching up wounds and putting a leader back on his feet again. Sometimes a spouse will act like a cheerleader, expressing confidence and admiration for a leader's abilities. How much better leaders can serve the Lord with this versatile staff member behind the scenes, helping the show go on!

Sometimes Church leaders become so overwhelmed they wish they were two people, or perhaps they wish they could clone themselves. Having a supportive spouse is even better than being two people. You think differently from your spouse, and that can be an advantage. He already knows what's in his head. With your insights, he knows even more than he did before. When asking a penny for your thoughts, your beloved companion might discover two heads are more valuable than one.

The Lord told Adam it was not good for man to be alone, and that is why he provided a "help meet" for him (see Genesis 2:18). What a wonderful word, *helpmeet*. Whenever I hear that word I picture hands. I picture wrinkled and well-worn hands at the ends of tanned arms, working, helping, serving along with the arms. Think of the absolute necessity of hands in accomplishing virtually every task you undertake. The hands essentially *help* the body *meet* its goals. You could literally say a helpmeet *helps* her spouse *meet* his goals.

Sometimes you may feel wrinkled and weathered like the capable, helping hands that belong to a "helpmeet." Every age spot and every wrinkle represents your valuable experience, your wisdom, and your dedicated support through years of service in which you and your spouse have been engaged.

The testimonies borne by brethren newly called to various assignments invariably pay tribute to their supportive spouses. Newly called general authorities and presidents of the Church's colleges always express appreciation for the support of their wives when accepting a new assignment or passing along an old assignment. You can read of their devotion to their wives in case after case. A humble man once admitted, "Behind every good man there is a good woman."

Providing this loving support such as the Brethren attribute to their wives may seem like a challenge only a saint can master. You may feel like the patient, understanding men and women who stand beside our Church leaders possess qualities that are almost impossible to emulate. In reality, supportive spouses of Church leaders come to understand their roles line upon line. We can all develop patience, understanding, and any other qualities of a supportive spouse as we learn and grow.

A TESTIMONY OF YOUR SPOUSE'S CALLING

You will find it incrementally easier to support your spouse in his or her Church calling when you have a strong testimony of that specific calling. You may already have a strong testimony of service, but supporting your spouse will prove far easier if you have a testimony not just of service in general but of your spouse's calling in particular. If your wife is called to serve as a Primary president, it will help if you seek a testimony of teaching your children correct principles at an early age. If your husband is called to serve as a Scoutmaster, try to gain a testimony of Scouting. If your spouse is called to work in the Family History Center, you may want to develop a testimony of family history. You probably love serving in your own little corner of the vineyard and already have a strong testimony of the area in which you serve, but when you develop a love for your spouse's corner of the vineyard too, you will be able to provide even greater support.

Supportive husbands and wives find it a lot easier to send their spouses away for the evening—even though they long to spend time together—if they know they are contributing to a good cause. Therefore, you will have an easier time supporting your spouse if you develop a love for the specific cause in which your spouse serves. Without a love for the specific cause in which your spouse serves, you might *hope* he or she is leaving for a good cause; you might have *faith* that your spouse would never leave you unless it was for a good cause. But when you grow to love the people your spouse serves, whether they are tiny children or elderly adults, you will *enthusiastically* send your spouse off to serve because *you* want to help them as much as your spouse does.

President Benson once said, "If we do not feel like praying, then we should pray until we do feel like praying" (*The Teachings of Ezra Taft Benson* [Salt Lake City: Bookcraft, 1988], 428). That sage advice contains so much wisdom. If you don't have a testimony of the gospel, you are instructed to experiment upon the word of God until it becomes delicious (see Alma 32:27–28). If you exercise even a particle of faith, your testimony will grow until it becomes strong. In a similar way, if *act* as if you have a burning testimony of your spouse's calling and feel a deep love for the people he or she serves, in time you will. Let your spouse's cause become your cause and you will find that supporting your spouse comes as naturally as breathing.

One of the first things I learned about my future husband before we married is that he had run a marathon. Never having run more than a mile myself, I was thoroughly impressed with anyone who could run 26.2 miles straight. I figured that was a really cool accomplishment to brag about the rest of his life. He would hang his medal on the wall, wear his marathon T-shirt until it was threadbare, and the marathon would be history.

After our marriage, I was dismayed to discover than running a marathon was not just a one-time "show how macho you can be" event. Running was a *hobby*. Not only did my husband want to run another marathon, he wanted to run all the time, all over the country!

I balked steadily about the time he spent running. He ran early in the morning and for hours on Saturday. Often he came home exhausted. After a marathon he would sometimes vomit. In one marathon his chest began to bleed, having been rubbed raw by his shirt for so long. I begged him to stop running so much. I suggested that perhaps he was overdoing it.

My comments reached the point where I could accurately be called a nag. And I didn't like it. I needed to accept the fact that my husband actually enjoyed running. He was going to continue running in spite of my objections. This ship was sailing with or without me, so I might as well jump aboard. I decided to try and support him.

When he came home with yet another pair of expensive running shoes, I started asking questions about the features that made them such wonderful shoes—a little sarcastically at first. ("How can anybody in their right mind justify asking so much money for a single pair of shoes?") Then I started looking for sales on these expensive products. My conversion didn't occur overnight; but eventually I took up running myself.

Once I paced him on foot for the last eight miles of his marathon. Another time I paced him on a bicycle for the entire marathon. Frequently when he ran a marathon, the children and I found spots along the route and we shouted encouragement to all the runners, giving them high fives and cheers. I can honestly say I began to love attending marathons. I became inspired, even awestruck, and completely respectful of the dedication of the participants.

I feel my life is richer now because I broadened my perspective and gained a new view on running. Bret and I now can have an animated conversation about running gear, routes, weather, and (after twenty-plus years of aging) the aches and pains caused and cured by running. Enjoying this sport together has proven a delightful addition to our relationship. At last my husband feels supported, not nagged. And I feel closer to him now that I have learned to see his view and truly value his perspective. His cause has become my cause.

The same kind of "at oneness" can occur between spouses who want to see eye-to-eye on the importance of Church service. You can become your spouse's biggest cheerleader and most loyal fan. You can cheer him on when he grows discouraged. You can encourage her when she feels inadequate. You can stand by his side when he feels alone. You can bear testimony when she needs a reminder of the reasons we serve. If you want to feel the same way your spouse does about his or her calling, merely open your mind, expand your thinking, and try to view your spouse's responsibilities the way he does.

Naturally, if you are going to be such a wonderful support to your spouse, you must take exceptional care of yourself. You can't give water from an empty well. Rest assured, the next section of this book discusses ways to make certain your own needs are met. This way you will have the stamina to support your spouse. As you ponder these pages on lifting your spouse's load, have faith that before long you will be clearly shown how to ensure your own needs are met as well.

THE NEED FOR ENCOURAGEMENT

You might imagine that Church leaders remain upbeat all of the time. Certainly when you see them on Sunday they seem to have their acts totally together. As your spouse serves, however, you may discover that there are times when he or she grows discouraged. Your sweetheart might feel overwhelmed by the magnitude of the work to be done. Your sweetheart might feel discouraged by the seeming lack of resources to do the work. Your sweetheart might despair because high expectations are not met. When you are available to listen, the person you love so dearly will reveal this discouragement.

Throughout the ages, even prophets have been discouraged by the demands of their assignments. Nephi chided himself, "Why should my heart weep and my soul linger in the valley of sorrow, and my flesh waste away, and my strength slacken, because of mine afflictions?" (2 Nephi 4:26). Mormon records the dilemma he felt regarding his ministry: "Behold, I am laboring with them continually; and when I speak the word of God with sharpness they tremble and anger against me; and when I use no sharpness they harden their hearts against it; wherefore, I fear lest the Spirit of the Lord hath ceased striving with them" (Moroni 9:4). Joseph Smith cried out, "O God, where art thou? And where is the pavilion that covereth thy hiding place?" (D&C 121:1).

You can prove to be an indispensable resource to your spouse as he or she endures the daily rigors of discipleship. Express your faith that any challenges your beloved faces will be overcome with the Lord's help. Remember that ups and downs are a part of life. No one gets a life full of downs. The downs may be the most disconcerting. But rest assured that what goes down will also come up. Discouraging times will not last. Wonderful times lie ahead. Life has its ups and downs. Not just its downs.

Don't despair that your spouse will meet an obstacle that cannot be overcome. It won't happen. This is the Lord's work. If we are asked to perform it, the Lord will provide a way. We can read throughout the scriptures about miracles that occur when servants of the Lord are about his work. We have seen miracles in recent years that demonstrate the vitality of the Lord's work. The Church's very existence is a looming testimony that the Lord's work will succeed.

You are in a unique position because you see the daily ups and downs of your spouse's calling. Even a priesthood leader or a counselor in a presidency does not see your spouse's challenges as regularly as you do. You know what your spouse is going through more thoroughly than anyone. Your spouse will undoubtedly reveal more intimate feelings to you than to anyone else. It's an honor and a privilege to be an available resource when a servant of the Lord needs some support.

At 9:00 one Sunday evening my husband walked through the door. His tie hung loosely around his unbuttoned collar and his hair was disheveled.

"How was your day?" I asked cheerily.

"I need a stair-hug," is all he said.

I scuttled to the staircase and stepped up one stair. I was then almost tall enough to look him in the eyes. He wrapped his arms around me, rested his head on my shoulder, and didn't say a word.

Eight hours earlier, during testimony meeting, our stake president had borne testimony of my husband's calling. "I was part of the process," he had said. "I know he is the Lord's choice to lead this ward." Several ward members had shared their testimonies too. They testified how the bishop had been inspired by the Spirit to give them the guidance they needed at critical times. As I sat in the congregation, my husband seemed bigger than life, like the bishops of my youth, who I thought could do no wrong. And here he was, eight hours later, seeking comfort, resting his head on my shoulder.

How I wished I were a foot or two taller.

CHAPTER 3

EQUALLY YOKED

DO YOU REMEMBER WHEN YOU WERE A CHILD and you used to run in a three-legged race? Two children paired up together, stood side by side with their inside legs tied together, then raced toward the finish line. Tall children could be paired up with short children, heavy children with light children. Runners inevitably tripped and fell. Sometimes a faster runner would literally drag his partner alongside him to finish the race. You learned quickly that the secret to winning a three-legged race was not to choose the fastest competitor out there as your companion. The secret to winning a three-legged race was to find a companion with whom you could stay in sync. When you are tied to someone who steps at the same pace you step, neither of you stumbles, and you rapidly complete the race.

The three-legged race must have been invented a really, really long time ago, during the days when oxen pulled covered wagons, because the game's strategy seems to have been copied by someone watching oxen pull wagons.

Two people who can run a three-legged race and stay in sync with one another are much like oxen that are tied together with a yoke and pull a wagon together. Both oxen need to pull in the same direction and at the same speed for the wagon to progress. If one ox refuses to pull, the other must wait around until the first ox decides to work. If one ox pulls the wagon at a fast pace and the other ox pulls the wagon at a slow pace, the wagon will go around in circles or even topple over on its side. It doesn't matter whether both oxen are naturally slow or both are naturally fast; the wagon will still progress forward as long as both oxen pull at the same rate. The wagon will move slower if both oxen are slow, but at least it will move forward.

In his second epistle to the Corinthians, Paul said, "Be ye not unequally yoked together with unbelievers: for what fellowship hath righteousness with unrighteousness? and what communion hath light with darkness?" (2 Corinthians 6:14).

Paul's metaphor of being equally yoked is meant for husbands and wives. A husband and wife are equally yoked when both pull the "wagon" at the same rate. Being equally yoked, in terms of Church service, means a husband and wife both have the same goals, those goals hold equal importance for both husband and wife, and the couple is headed the same direction. Both want the same thing for their family, for the Church, for mankind.

MARRYING WITHIN THE COVENANT

The Lord was so concerned that the Israelites who were settling in Canaan marry those with whom they were equally yoked that he actually commanded the Israelites to destroy the inhabitants of the land they were to occupy, lest the covenant people intermarry with the Gentiles:

"And when the Lord thy God shall deliver them before thee;

thou shalt smite them, and utterly destroy them; thou shalt make no covenant with them, nor shew mercy unto them:

"Neither shalt thou make marriages with them; thy daughter thou shalt not give unto his son, nor his daughter shalt thou take unto thy son.

"For they will turn away thy son from following me, that they may serve other gods: so will the anger of the Lord be kindled against you, and destroy thee suddenly" (Deuteronomy 7:2–4).

Marrying someone who was not his spiritual equal destroyed Solomon's testimony:

"But king Solomon loved many strange women, together with the daughter of Pharaoh, women of the Moabites, Ammonites, Edomites, Zidonians, and Hittites;

"Of the nations concerning which the Lord said unto the children of Israel, Ye shall not go in to them, neither shall they come in unto you: for surely they will turn away your heart after their gods: Solomon clave unto these in love. . . .

"For it came to pass, when Solomon was old, that his wives turned away his heart after other gods" (1 Kings 11:1–2, 4).

THE UNEQUALLY YOKED

Just as in the days of Moses and in the days of Paul, today the characteristics of a spouse can significantly influence an individual's ability to serve in the kingdom. A spouse who places demands on the servant of the Lord that conflict with his or her ability to serve will certainly hamper a servant's effectiveness. Consider the sister who is married to a nonmember who strongly desires her company at professional football games on Sunday. Every other year, when her ward meets in the afternoon, she misses church to keep harmony in her marriage.

Occasionally a Latter-day Saint marries someone who can't

imagine why we must spend three hours at church each Sunday. These members are often forced to choose which of the three meetings they will attend in order to cause their spouse the least distress.

Like oxen who are unequally yoked, a husband who lags far behind his wife in spiritual matters can slow the wife down spiritually, and a wife who lags far behind her husband in spiritual matters can slow the husband down spiritually.

BALANCING ONE ANOTHER

Husbands and wives have a tendency to become more like one another as they continue their relationship. A righteous spouse may become more like an unrighteous spouse, as was the case with King Solomon. Similarly, an unrighteous spouse can become more like a righteous spouse.

You may have marveled that some couples come to look like one another over time. We joke about a husband gaining "sympathy weight" when his wife is pregnant. The science of biology refers to this principle as "structural coupling." According to this concept, "the more we repeatedly interact with someone or something over time, the more we become like that person or thing" (Wendy L. Watson, *Purity and Passion* [Salt Lake City: Deseret Book, 2001], 84). Science seems to confirm the hunch that husbands and wives tend to become more like one another over time.

If you have ever watched a couple who are talented dancers perform together, you notice how uniformly they move. They seem to read one another's minds; they stay in such perfect sync. With practice, and over time, these artists learn to perform with unity. A man and woman who dance together, paying attention to each other's moves and blending into each other's pace, create beauty that will inspire and awe.

A couple who are equally yoked, working in sync to carry forth the work of the Lord, can inspire us all. When both members of a couple come into the marriage with strong testimonies of the gospel, they each engage in personal scripture study and prayer. Both repent daily and strive to better live the gospel. Both the husband and the wife are motivated to serve the Lord, and they do a tremendous amount of good in the world.

Husbands and wives who begin a marriage with different levels of spiritual commitment have the opportunity to become more like one another as they continue their marriage. Like talented dancers—with practice and over time—theirs can become a marriage of equals as they grow more like one another.

KEEPING UP WITH YOUR SPOUSE

The way to achieve unity in a marriage when one member is soaring spiritually and the other is lagging is twofold. The soaring partner can slow down, or the lagging partner can speed up. By doing either, the couple will pull the wagon together and not work against one another. Of course, if the lagging spouse chooses to speed up, the companionship will more effectively contribute to the work of the kingdom, and the individual who increases in spirituality will attain the personal rewards of righteous living.

Church leaders, of necessity, keep themselves spiritually in tune so they can receive inspiration in their callings. They spend much time in prayer and in pondering the scriptures. In addition, a valiant servant will have many testimony-strengthening experiences as a result of the service rendered in the kingdom. Spirituality increases as a natural result of magnifying one's calling. All this can leave the spouse of a valiant Church servant, who watches the servant grow in spirituality, feeling as though he or she is being left behind in the Church servant's spiritual dust.

Should a supportive spouse desire to be equally yoked with a Church leader who is enjoying spiritual experiences, he or she can achieve that goal by deliberately strengthening and building his or her individual testimony. None of us needs to wait until we receive a calling to begin spiritual growth. Spiritual growth can occur readily when an individual is obedient, fasts, prays, and studies the scriptures diligently and ponders and prays about the contents.

I am particularly convinced that spiritual growth comes from reading the scriptures. Spiritual growth seems to occur regardless of what I read, but simply *because* I read. I find that the Holy Ghost whispers truth to my mind when I simply open and study holy writ. I may receive the answer to a question that doesn't even relate to the chapter and verse I am reading. When you are in a receptive frame of mind and are pondering and doing the Lord's will, it is a perfect time for him to bless you with personal revelation. It seems the Lord blesses his children with spiritual insight simply because they are obedient enough to pause sometime during the day and put themselves in a receptive frame of mind. Just as being in church puts you in a position to feel the Spirit because you are where the Lord wants you to be on the Sabbath day, reading the scriptures is where the Lord wants you to be at some time each day. It's like being in the right place at the right time—your mind is in a mental place that is receptive to the Spirit. By putting yourself in a receptive frame of mind, you give yourself an opportunity to hear the Lord's answers to your prayers.

SLOW AND STEADY WINS THE RACE

Remember the analogy of the three-legged race? One interesting thing about contestants in a three-legged race is that the pair that wins the race is not always the pair with the fastest runner. The pair that wins the race is the pair that works well together. A pair of three-legged race contestants can improve their performance when the slower runner increases his speed in order to keep up with the faster runner, or partners can improve their performance when the faster runner slows down just enough that the slower runner can keep pace. Naturally, two fast runners will cover a lot more ground than two medium-paced runners, but two medium-paced runners and even two slow runners will cover more ground than a pair that is so unequal they keep tripping one another.

This principle of unity exists in a marriage, too. You have a choice about whether or not to keep up spiritually with your spouse. Even if you don't sprint, you can get along with your mate perfectly fine if you stay together spiritually and grow at a comfortable rate. As long as a husband and wife are both headed in the same direction, the speed with which they travel doesn't matter as much as the fact that they progress along the path. As Elder Neal A. Maxwell said, "God is still more concerned with growth than geography" (*Notwithstanding My Weakness* [Salt Lake City: Bookcraft, 1981], 11).

Ideally, a husband and wife will both work hard on their own spiritual growth because it not only unifies them but also helps them to do tremendous good in furthering the work of the kingdom. If unity is lacking in a marriage, finding a pace that is comfortable for both the husband and wife will restore that unity. The couple will keep moving forward, even if they aren't the fastest runners in the race.

Quarreling between husband and wife most assuredly slows progress. If the spouse who runs at a breakneck pace slows down and runs in step with his partner, he will make it farther faster than he will dragging her along and causing them both to trip and stumble. An ambitious, enthusiastic servant may delight in the work of the kingdom. However, by establishing unity in the marriage and then progressing at a pace that is comfortable for both husband and wife, he will fare better in the long run than he will by running ahead and causing resentment at home.

"It doesn't do any good to be the first one at the pearly gates if you arrive alone," a bishop once said. "You want your mate with you in the celestial kingdom anyway, so you might as well be patient and go together."

The scriptures remind us over and over again to make sure we have good feelings about our fellowman before we attempt to embark on the service of the Lord. In the Sermon on the Mount the Savior teaches, "Therefore if thou bring thy gift to the altar, and there rememberest that thy brother hath ought against thee; Leave there thy gift before the altar, and go thy way; first be reconciled to thy brother, and then come and offer thy gift" (Matthew 5:23–24).

In applying this scripture to yourself, you learn that before going out and serving your fellowman through fulfilling Church callings, you should make an effort to assure that your relationships with your "brother" or spouse or children are harmonious.

Recall what happened one day when the Prophet Joseph Smith was cross with Emma. The Prophet was unable to proceed with the translation of the Book of Mormon until he mended his relationship with his wife. We learn a phenomenal lesson from Brother Joseph. As important as the work was (could there possibly be anything more important than translating the Book of Mormon in restoring the gospel to the earth?), unity in the Prophet's marriage took precedence. The Lord was willing to actually halt the work while Joseph restored harmony in his marriage (see *Best-Loved Stories of the LDS People*, ed. Jack M.

Lyon, Linda Ririe Gundry, and Jay A. Parry [Salt Lake City: Deseret Book, 1997], 35).

SIDE BY SIDE

We all know that a missionary who wants to rise early, follow the mission rules to a tee, study the scriptures as a companionship, and fill unscheduled hours finding contacts experiences considerable exasperation when paired up with a companion who sleeps late, disobeys the mission rules, or refuses to accompany his companion to important appointments. Like husbands and wives, missionary companions accomplish more together when they are equally yoked.

Full-time missionaries must achieve unity with their companions in order to fulfill one aspect of the Church's mission, to share the gospel. Husbands and wives who serve in the stakes and wards of Zion achieve unity in order to fill another aspect of the Church's threefold mission, perfecting the Saints.

You have the opportunity, just like the elders and the sisters who serve full-time, to find a pace that suits both you and your companion so you can both progress smoothly in your service to mankind and in your quest for eternal life.

While visiting Preston, England, some time ago, I took the opportunity to meet some friends at the Missionary Training Center. Directly adjacent to the MTC, the grounds of the temple gleamed a rolling-hills green. Elderly couples walked along sidewalks flanked with colorful flowerbeds. George and Julie Collins were just finishing companion scripture study as they welcomed me into their apartment.

"This mission is the best thing that ever happened to us," Julie beamed. "Our relationship is stronger than it's ever been."

Another sister I met, a petite blonde, who stood next to her very silver-haired husband, said, "We never dreamed we could have so much fun. We are enjoying one another more than we have in years."

Senior couples who serve missions together frequently find that, along with their love for the gospel, their love for one another grows. Working together towards the same righteous goals brings unity in their relationship and strengthens their testimonies. They pray for the same investigators; they pine over the same lost sheep. Their talents frequently complement one another and magnify their effectiveness.

If you and your spouse are together engaged in the work of perfecting the Saints, you can expect your relationship to grow stronger and richer as you serve side by side, pursuing the same goal as your beloved. Your love for one another will grow as your love for the gospel grows. And you don't even have to wait until you retire for it to happen.

Different Strengths, Identical Values

An equally yoked couple need not possess the very same strengths. A husband and a wife may each possess very different strengths that they will use in service to the Lord. A husband may be gregarious and outgoing, and a wife may be shy and sensitive. Just because they possess different strengths doesn't mean they are progressing at different rates. It's easy to confuse different strengths with different values. A couple is equally yoked when both maintain similar values and place those values in the same place on a list of priorities. Couples grow apart when their lists of values don't match.

If both husband and wife place the family first on their list of priorities, and both husband and wife place Church service second, harmony will abound. However, if a husband places

Church service on the top of his list of values, and the wife places the family on the top of her list of values, this may cause some contention. The fact that their values *differ* creates conflict.

A couple will experience unity, for example, if they both value tidiness, or both value time together but can tolerate some disarray. Conflict occurs when one member of a couple is hardworking and the other lazy, or when one saves and the other spends. Conflict can even result when one spouse is a "morning person" and the other enjoys staying up later at night. Unity occurs when their goals and values coincide.

A Boost to Your Marriage

A husband and wife who are unified in their values can "set the mission on fire." Whether they are serving a full-time mission together proclaiming the gospel, or whether their mission is to perfect the Saints, there is nothing more unifying, more exciting, or healthier for a marriage than to be working together toward the same goals and succeeding. It is exhilarating. It brings you closer together and strengthens the bonds of love in a way all the second honeymoons in the world could not do.

I remember a time a seminary class I was teaching was nearing the end of the school year, and I still hadn't taught the last twelve books of the Old Testament. I was beginning to panic and I shared my concern with my husband. The following conversation ensued:

JeaNette: "I'm cutting this so close that I'm afraid my students will be walking out the door while I'm trying to teach our last scripture-mastery verse."

Bret: "I can imagine. They will be trying to close the door of the car and you'll put your foot in the door and say: 'Behold, I will send you Elijah the prophet before the coming of the great and dreadful day of the Lord.'"

JeaNette: "They will start to drive away and I'll have to yell after them, 'And he shall turn the heart of the fathers to the children, and the heart of the children to their fathers . . .'"

Bret: "You will be chasing after them in your high heels: '. . . lest I come and smite the earth with a curse.'"

We burst into laughter at the hilarity of the scene. Our intimacy grew because he knew exactly how I felt. He even knew the subject I would be teaching at the last minute. He knew it well enough to quote the scripture with me. We felt like an elderly couple who have lived together such a long time, they find themselves saying the same thing at the same time. We truly felt of one heart and one mind.

CHAPTER 4

THE TRUE MEANING
OF SUPPORT

DURING THE TIME MY HUSBAND SERVED AS BISHOP
my father died. While serving a couples' mission in Manchester,
England, Dad fell backward, hit his head at the base of the skull,
and slipped into a coma before he ever arrived at the hospital.

I flew to England to see my father, helped make arrangements
to transport him back to his home in Salt Lake City, then
returned to Florida. However, before the plane left England to
bring Dad home to the United States, he died. So I packed up the
children, hopped on another plane, and flew to Salt Lake City for
the funeral.

Transporting an individual who had died from a head injury
proved even more complicated than transporting an individual in
a coma, and it took ten days for Dad's body to arrive in Utah.
Eventually we had the funeral and I returned to Florida. All in all,
I was out of commission for about a month.

During my absence, my husband stayed busy rendering
Church service in Florida. He spent his evenings visiting the

less-active and home teaching those who hadn't been home taught for a while. He reorganized the Young Women organization. On Easter Sunday he invited all the single men in our ward over for dinner—and for the first time in his life, he baked a ham.

When I heard about all this activity, I assumed my husband was relieved that I was out of town. He probably wished I would stay a little longer so he could concentrate on our ward members. He didn't have anybody to return home to at the end of the day, so he could continue serving at this frenzied pace and chip his "to do" list down to a single page.

When I finally came home I felt the need to apologize, not for being away but for coming back! Now along with all Bret's ecclesiastical responsibilities, he had a grieving wife to comfort. I worried that I would be another burden.

Boy, did I worry wrong. "I feel terribly selfish telling you this, JeaNette," Bret began. "I know that you've been really busy since your father's death, but I need you here." Then he burst into tears. I watched speechless as he sobbed. His head hung over his body as if he were twice his forty-one years of age. He turned his cheek into his starched white shirt and wiped his face on the sleeve. "I can't serve in my calling without you," he finally managed to whisper. "You're the only who truly understands."

Ice-cold water poured over my head would not have startled me out of my stupor more effectively. An angel could have appeared at that moment and I would not have even gasped. Before that day, I figured the support of a spouse was important. But I didn't really understand what it *meant* to support your spouse.

I learned that support does not mean that you stay out of the way and take a back seat. Support does not mean that you keep your mouth shut. Support does not mean that you refrain from complaining. Support does not mean that you hold in all your feelings and refuse to add to your spouse's burden.

A spouse is not a burden on the back of a busy Church leader. A spouse can be the wings on the back of the Lord's servant, helping him feel as if he can fly, walk on water, or ace whatever assignment he is given. In the words of Bette Midler, a spouse can provide "the wind beneath [his] wings."

What does a spouse offer that makes such a huge difference in a leader's ability to serve? Why hadn't Bret felt *less* burdened in my absence, as I thought he would? How did my return lighten his load? What exactly does a spouse offer a valiant Church leader that helps him serve to his full ability?

A bishop stood at the podium in a ward we lived in long ago. He sang his wife's praises because, as much as he was gone, she never complained. He said in all his years as bishop his wife had never said a *single* word about the long hours he kept and the time he spent away from home. I remember sitting in the pews feeling my face burn as he spoke, because my husband was his elders quorum president, and I had said more than a *single* word about the hours my husband spent away from our family.

Not long afterward this bishop quit. He literally quit. He failed to show up to church one Sunday and he has not been back since. It dawned on me that simply remaining mute about the time a spouse spends in Church service may not necessarily be the definition of support. For twenty years I thought husbands and wives could best support the devoted Church servant in their home by merely staying out of the way and letting them "do their thing," whatever that may be.

I learned that nothing could be further from the truth. Support does not mean that you as a spouse should stay away, leave the servant alone, and mind your own business. Support means that you become involved, work side by side, jump in and take part in the work, allow the work of the Lord to be a priority to you *both*. Remaining mute and avoiding complaints will, at times, be a necessary requirement for supporting a devoted Church servant, but it is not sufficient. Certainly a Church leader will appreciate not being brought down by a complaining spouse. However, a supportive spouse not only avoids bringing a Church leader down but also works to lift him up.

Although the beloved Church leader whom you support will have many wonderfully fulfilling experiences as a servant of the Lord, he or she will also have many difficult experiences. A supportive spouse holds the leader up; like the supports beneath a bridge or the I-beams in a building, a supportive spouse helps the leader stand in his place.

BEARING ANOTHER'S BURDENS THAT THEY MAY BE LIGHT

Alma teaches us how to support one another in a very familiar passage in Mosiah. Typically when we read this passage we apply it to the sheep within the flock. We bear one another's burdens that they may be light, we mourn with those that mourn, we comfort those who stand in need of comfort. Try, as you read Alma's words, to apply them to the shepherd of the flock. Imagine bearing the burdens of the shepherd you married.

"And it came to pass that he said unto them: Behold, here are the waters of Mormon (for thus were they called) and now, as ye are desirous to come unto the fold of God, and to be called his people, and are willing to bear one another's burdens, that they may be light;

"Yea, and are willing to mourn with those that mourn; yea, and comfort those that stand in need of comfort, and to stand as witnesses of God at all times and in all things, and in all places that ye may be in, even until death, that ye may be redeemed of God, and be numbered with those of the first resurrection, that ye may have eternal life—

"Now I say unto you, if this be the desire of your hearts, what have you against being baptized in the name of the Lord, as a witness before him that ye have entered into a covenant with him, that ye will serve him and keep his commandments, that he may pour out his Spirit more abundantly upon you?" (Mosiah 18:8–10).

What brilliant counsel Alma provides when we apply his words to our spouses! We all know that joining the fold of God gives us an opportunity to bear our fellow Saints' burdens. But what about the burdens of our beloved companions?

Who in your congregation are you in a better position to mourn with than your sweetheart? Who in your congregation can you comfort as effectively as you can the person you married?

The unity that binds the members of the wards and stakes of Zion, the unity that is created when we bear one another's burdens that they may be light—that unity begins in the homes of our members as we each lovingly and tenderly bear the burdens of those we married.

A Variety of Burdens

Some of the burdens your spouse bears are physical burdens: moving people in, giving people rides, cleaning up after events, and so on. I will review how to support your spouse with the tangible, physical burdens later in this book. However, the burdens that cause your spouse the greatest concern are not likely to be physical burdens. Emotional burdens, such as feeling inadequate, overwhelmed, or discouraged, weigh down a Church leader to a far greater degree than do the physical burdens.

Some may find it hard to imagine that any of the capable leaders who carry forth this great work could ever feel inadequate to the task. However, if you talk to them, read their writings, and listen to their testimonies, you will inevitably hear them express abject humility at the awesome responsibility of bringing salvation to human souls. Prophets both ancient and modern reveal their self-doubt when such a looming task is presented them. These men and women receive no professional training. They do not attend divinity school. They do not carry degrees in theology. The world has not pronounced them qualified to teach the gospel of Jesus Christ. But Jesus Christ himself has. How comforting it must be, when filled with feelings of inadequacy, to have a trusted, beloved spouse express confidence in the abilities the leader doubts and to maintain faith in the Lord's constant guidance.

Though it's hard to imagine Church leaders feeling inadequate, it's not difficult to imagine them feeling overwhelmed. The work load Church leaders carry would daunt a man with Samson's strength. Most of the leaders in The Church of Jesus Christ of Latter-day Saints volunteer their services and, of necessity, simultaneously maintain a full-time, income-producing job. Trying to support a family while fulfilling the responsibilities accompanying a demanding ecclesiastical position can leave a Church leader feeling buried under heavy burdens. Again, a spouse's willingness to lift burdens that are within her power to lift and her testimony that the Lord will strengthen the backs of his faithful servants can give an overwhelmed Church leader courage to proceed.

Our mission as members of the Church is to proclaim the gospel, perfect the Saints, and redeem the dead. Although we don't always know whether the dead are accepting the gospel, we personally witness the acceptance or rejection of those whom we teach on this earth. Watching people reject the gospel when it is such a valuable gift can be very difficult. Can you imagine Church leaders becoming discouraged at times?

Servants of the Lord who valiantly work to fulfill their commission as leaders of men will feel as if their hearts are being torn in two (rent) when some do not heed the cry to repent.

Throughout the scriptures we read the lamentations of tireless prophets of God who continually cry repentance unto the people, then have their hearts ache when the people remain in wickedness.

Nephi said, "My soul is rent with anguish because of you, and my heart is pained" (1 Nephi 17:47). Mormon said, "And my soul was rent with anguish, because of the slain of my people, and I cried: O ye fair ones, how could ye have departed from the ways of the Lord!" (Mormon 6:16–17). The three Nephite Apostles who chose not to taste of death were promised that they should have no pain, "save it be for the sins of the world" (3 Nephi 28:9). The sins of the world are a timeless cause for mourning.

Alma beautifully teaches us how we can bear the emotional burdens of our loved ones. Whether our loved ones are discouraged because they feel inadequate, overwhelmed, or discouraged, we can bear the emotional burdens of our loved ones when we "mourn with those that mourn . . . and comfort those that stand in need of comfort" (Mosiah 18:9).

You hold the privileged position, a position no other can hold, to be the one your sweetheart comes home to. You are the one who will open your arms and invite him to rest his head on your shoulder and put up his feet. You have the honor of providing respite for one of the Lord's chosen servants.

A supportive spouse does not need to bake a fancy dinner, or fill the house with roses, or give a lengthy foot massage to bear her loved one's burdens. She need only allow the burdened to share his feelings, care deeply that the burdened has those feelings, and express confidence in the leader and faith in the Lord's willingness to aid his cause.

You may not need to utter a word to let your busy Church leader know that you support him, you care deeply, and are concerned about his or her feelings. Your jaw may drop and your mouth hang slightly open while your spouse expresses himself. Your rapt focus, the expression on your face, and your willingness to put everything aside for the moment and give your spouse your undivided attention will all communicate your heartfelt concern. Should you respond with a reverent, "Wow!" that will be enough to tell your spouse you care and that his feelings matter to you.

Naturally, your spouse will enjoy many delightful, happy experiences while serving the Lord. I will later discuss the importance of sharing triumphs with one another. Negative emotions, however, tend to spill out more readily than positive ones for someone who feels inadequate, discouraged, or overwhelmed. Holding in these negative emotions can make a person feel like they are going to explode, so they may seek out a listening ear more readily when a negative experience occurs than when a positive experience occurs.

NO ONE LIKE YOU

You are in a unique position to provide emotional support to your spouse. Church leaders experience challenging situations every single day. The beauty of sharing with a husband or wife is that they are a daily part of the Church servant's life. A spouse can keep up with struggles and the joys as they occur. A spouse can share feelings in all the poignancy of the moment, without the disadvantage of time creeping between the emotion and the spouse's expressing it. This immediacy allows the Church leader to convey the depth of his feelings while the feelings are still deep.

Furthermore, no one on the planet loves your spouse as much as you. No one would be as devastated if he or she were in trouble, or as elated over a promotion, or as concerned for his or her health, or as delighted by daily, personal victories. Because you are of one heart, your heart breaks for your spouse when he or she is in pain, and it can overflow with joy when your spouse experiences a triumph.

A husband or wife can generally show greater understanding of the person they married because they know their spouse's personality better than anyone else does. A spouse knows why certain situations affect the leader in a particular manner. A spouse knows why some situations cause more distress than others; and a spouse knows why the leader may react differently than another leader might under the same circumstances.

Wilford Farnsworth Jr., who has served as both a regional representative and a mission president, credits his wife for keeping him going through hard times. "She inspired and lifted me when I was down or discouraged, shared my sorrows, and rejoiced with me as our missionaries honored their priesthood and their calls. For the first time in our lives, we were in all ways together.

"I can't even conceive of accepting such a call as that [mission president] without someone like my wife at my side," President Farnsworth says. "We were constant companions during that period and were truly partners. Yes, I was the mission president, but she was my principal confidante and counselor" (Wilford M. Farnsworth Jr., in "Equal Partners: Two Versions," in *Women and the Power Within,* ed. Dawn Hall Anderson and Marie Cornwall [Salt Lake City: Deseret Book, 1991], 109).

When you share feelings with another individual, it helps you bond. You learn about one another, you grow in appreciation for one another, and you grow to trust one another. Of all the relationships that could benefit from this kind of emotional intimacy, the marital relationship looms paramount. "If we're going to spend eternity with each other, we ought to know each other's thoughts, opinions, worries, frustrations, and hopes," said Sister Chris Gray when interviewed by her husband for an *Ensign* article titled "What I Learned about Serving My Wife" (*Ensign*, June 1995, 56).

One of the ways we create a celestial marriage, a marriage in which we are in all ways "at one," is to bear one another's burdens, to mourn with one another, and to comfort one another. Supporting a loved one in a Church calling is an ideal way to create the at-one-ness that defines a celestial marriage.

The Need to Talk

Bret alluded to the value of someone who could mourn with him and comfort him when, upon my return from my father's funeral, he lamented, "I didn't have anybody to talk to." Having someone with whom you can share poignant feelings is a blessing of tremendous worth.

I was intrigued by a movie that came out a while back called *Cast Away.* In the movie the hero learns to survive while stranded on a deserted island. He discovers that not only does he need food and shelter; he also needs someone to talk to. So desperate is he for companionship that he paints a face on a volleyball and names it Wilson; he shares his feelings with this volleyball. When he loses the volleyball, he is devastated. One of the many messages I took away from the film is that not having someone to share life with renders life unlivable.

I have always been deeply touched by the tender feelings shared by Mormon when he wrote to his son Moroni. Notice especially the affectionate way in which they communicate. It is apparent that these men are of one heart, unified in the work, and wholly supportive of one another. All of Moroni chapter eight is a treasure, but consider in these excerpts the *intense feelings,* as well as the *affection,* between men who can share such feelings with a like-minded brother in the gospel:

"My beloved son, Moroni, I rejoice exceedingly that your Lord Jesus Christ hath been mindful of you. . . .

"And now, my son, I speak unto you concerning that which grieveth me exceedingly; . . .

"And I am filled with charity, which is everlasting love; . . .

"Pray for them, my son, that repentance may come unto them. But behold, I fear lest the Spirit hath ceased striving with them" (vv. 2, 4, 17, 28).

Throughout the next chapter, Mormon pours out his heart in complete and utter anguish over the depravity of both the Nephites and the Lamanites. His pain is evident in every verse. Yet I still sense his affection for his son, whom he repeatedly addresses as "my son" or "my beloved son." As Mormon pours out his heart to his beloved son, I can feel the unity, the oneness between these two men engaged wholeheartedly in the same cause. Such unity reminds me of God the Father and *his* Beloved Son, Jesus Christ, both at one in their efforts to bring men unto salvation.

I can't help but contrast this feeling of unity to the abject loneliness Moroni records after his father dies. The horrid task of watching his brethren destroy one another is almost more than he can bear, and certainly more than he wants to bear alone:

"And my father also was killed by them, and I even remain alone to write the sad tale of the destruction of my people. But behold, they are gone, and I fulfill the commandment of my father. And whether they will slay me, I know not.

"Therefore I will write and hide up the records in the earth; and whither I go it mattereth not" (Mormon 8:3–4).

It almost seems that the support of his father kept Moroni going, and without his father he is so sad that nothing matters anymore.

The opportunity a leader has to share feelings with someone who truly cares about their plight, with whom they are of one mind, makes it possible to bear the burdens that are placed upon the servants of the Lord.

Although we hope we will never witness the physical carnage Mormon and Moroni witnessed, we may see spiritual carnage that is devastating to view. The support of a like-minded spouse will enable Church leaders to continue on in this great cause, although the challenges facing them can be at times discouraging.

A Young Women president felt overwhelmed by the challenges her young women were facing, and she felt totally inadequate about her ability to help them. She "vented" to her husband and later recalled, "Simply uttering my concerns out loud made them seem less enormous."

It goes without saying that it is inappropriate for a priesthood leader to share confidential matters with others—particularly not with a spouse. In fact, nothing will compromise a bishop's ability to effectively counsel with ward members more than a suspicion among the members that he is untrustworthy, that what he learns in interviews will become the topic of discussion at home. Besides, it is unfair to burden a spouse with information or concerns about which she can do nothing or to tell her something that will distort her view of someone in the ward. That said, there are some emotional benefits to be derived from counseling with a spouse.

1. He understands more clearly his experiences. By being forced to put his emotions into words, he can make sense of confusing emotions and can decide what to think of them.

2. He achieves emotional distance, so he can look from the outside in—kind of like watching a scary movie as opposed to having a bad dream. You know you'll make it through the movie; in a dream, you're not sure you'll make it through until you wake up.

3. He can look more objectively at the situation so he can see the event as having a place in the world but not filling up the whole world, or having a place in time but not lasting forever.

4. He perceives his concerns as more manageable when they can be identified, discussed, delegated, and passed back and forth between two people.

5. He recognizes that he has good reason to feel how he does when someone validates those feelings. He doesn't place unrealistic expectations upon himself to feel differently than he does.

6. He recognizes there are other things of import in this world, like the family member in front of him.

Truly feeling that someone cares deeply about his or her plight will significantly lighten the burden the Church leader carries. When a spouse agrees to mourn with those who mourn and comfort those who stand in need of comfort, two sets of shoulders carry the load, and it is only half as heavy.

You've Got It in You

Bearing one another's burdens may be easier than you think. You can provide support for your loved one simply by being there and showing you care. You don't have to say anything brilliant or come up with any clever solutions. Bearing another's burdens doesn't mean you take the burden away. It means you lend your back, and you carry the burden together.

Has one of your children ever come home all teary-eyed because the kids in the neighborhood wouldn't let him play with them? Your little one runs sobbing into the house, barely able to catch his breath. You quickly check for cuts or bruises and determine the problem does not require a visit to emergency room. Then your son blurts out, "They won't let me play . . ." At times like this, you discover that all the wise words in the world will fall on deaf ears. Your precious child doesn't want to hear about children being insensitive at times, or changing their minds from one day to the next. All he wants is for you to love him. He wants only to sit in your lap and be held. So you stroke his hair, and gently whisper, "Don't worry, it will be all right." Moments later he hops out of your lap, all better, and goes right back to the pack of children who shooed him away. Buoyed up and encouraged, he is ready to face the world again.

The gentle kindness you show toward a distressed son or daughter will be very much like that you would offer your distressed spouse. You don't have to offer any brilliant solutions. You don't have to extend words of wisdom. You need only express your confidence, your love, and your genuine caring for your beloved at this trying time.

Tremendous security comes from knowing that someone loves you to your very soul, no matter what challenges you face or how skillfully you handle them. Knowing that you are standing by his side will give your spouse the courage to go on.

Sharing Triumphs

Although it is important for an overwhelmed servant of the Lord to share the negative emotions he or she experiences, it is important to the marital relationship for the servant to share positive emotions too, lest the spouse become overwhelmed.

Perhaps you'll want to make this agreement with the beloved Church leader you support: agree to listen to all the frustrations and disappointments your spouse experiences. However, invite your spouse to share the triumphs and rewards of the calling as well. It is too difficult for a spouse to perceive a loved one as always being burdened. It makes our hearts ache. Learning about your spouse's successes as well as the challenges will help you put in truer perspective your spouse's experiences as a servant of the Lord.

While Bret was serving as bishop, an especially wonderful event occurred, which I was delighted he shared with me.

A young sailor I'll call Mark Smith had seen some of the Church's commercials on television and called a toll-free number to receive a free copy of *Our Heavenly Father's Plan.* The missionaries delivered the tape and invited Mark to take the discussions, which he did. He soon desired to be baptized. The day of his baptism Mark did not have transportation to the church, so he spent the last eight dollars in his wallet on a taxicab.

Bret was the elders quorum president of the ward in which Mark lived, so he immediately began to fellowship Brother Smith. We shared one of our family's favorite Christmas traditions with the Smith family: each Christmas we assemble a gingerbread house, and then select somebody new to take it to. Sometimes we have to make several houses before we produce one that can stand without collapsing, but eventually, with enough frosting and peppermints, we can keep the walls upright. We then sing Christmas carols at the door before presenting the gingerbread house. Brother Smith's wife was so touched by our tradition (not by the quality of our gingerbread house!) that she said she wanted a family like ours, and she soon started taking the discussions herself.

Before long the Smiths moved away. We also moved away,

and we did not hear from them for many years. However, a mutual friend reported that the Smiths had some subsequent trouble in their marriage and were considering a divorce.

Not long after this sad news, Brother Smith moved into our *new* ward, not the one we had lived in together previously; coincidentally, he moved into the same *new* ward we had moved into! Bret just happened to be the bishop of our new ward, and Brother Smith remembered Bret from when Bret had been his elders quorum president. Bret again began to serve Brother Smith, who, indeed, was separated from his wife. Several months of interviews went by and eventually the wife moved back in with her husband. Today the Smiths are both active in the Church, along with their four darling children, and have recently been sealed in the temple. Enjoying this miracle alongside my husband greatly encouraged me, and helped me accept that other experiences would send him home feeling discouraged and defeated.

Blessings for the Relationship

Sharing the joys and triumphs of a Church calling will bond you and your loved one together every bit as effectively as mourning together over the losses. A cupid's arrow couldn't spark the kind of affection that develops when you share intimate feelings with one another.

Sharing triumphs you experience while serving the Lord is somewhat like having a baby together. Each time one of your children is born, you and your spouse rejoice together. Your joy is multiplied because you have someone with which to share that joy—someone who feels as delighted as you do. Because you can share the feelings of being so blessed, so humbled, with someone else who feels equally blessed, equally humble, the experience is richer. You grow closer sharing this marvelous experience with one another.

Have you ever watched a shooting star, or a nest full of baby birds, or a whale in the wild spouting water so close you got wet? Do you remember how much you wanted to share your delight with someone? "Look, over there! Isn't that awesome?" you may exclaim. Life's positive experiences are richer when they are shared with someone who cares. In addition, life's challenges are more tolerable when they are shared with someone who cares.

CHAPTER 5

SELFLESS LISTENING

IF YOUR BELOVED COMPANION CAN FEEL THE LOAD fall from his back simply by sharing poignant emotions with you, he will feel lighter than air when he shares poignant emotions and not only do you respond with care and concern but you seem to truly understand where your spouse is coming from.

One husband described the feeling of being understood by his wife with the phrase, "She gets me." Although far from eloquent, that brief response clearly summarized the comfort of feeling understood by another human being. Two people grow in unity when they "get" one another—when they understand where the other person is coming from and why the other person feels as they do.

You can better understand your loved one, you can "get" him, when, in addition to listening with compassion and concern, you comprehend what it's like to be in his shoes.

LISTEN WITH YOUR HEART

The secret to truly understanding your loved one is listening with your heart. Listening with your heart is different than listening with your ears. When you listen with your ears, you hear what the other person *says*, but when you listen with your heart you discover what the other person *feels*.

In the Book of Mormon we find the word *heart* 147 times, and only five of those incidences refer to the organ in a man's chest that pumps blood through his body. In 142 cases, the Book of Mormon uses the heart to symbolize feelings, devotions, emotions, and loyalties.

When you listen with your heart, you listen with empathy, first trying to imagine how the other person feels and next what it's *like* to feel that way. Listening with your heart allows you to feel "at one" with your beloved. You can grow closer because you have made an effort to see into your companion's heart. This cannot be done with your eyes, only with your own heart.

Selfless Listening

A concrete way to practice listening with your heart is to listen selflessly. You can forget yourself for a moment and put yourself in another's shoes when you focus completely on the one sharing his feelings. Understanding can't occur if the listener can see the subject from only *his* (the listener's) point of view.

Allen Bergin, a professor at Brigham Young University, tells of an incident in which he set aside his own point of view and saw the world from his wife's point of view.

"One evening . . . , under the pressure of important work assignments, I left for the office. Although it was an important evening at home, because the autumn grape harvest was in and grape juice was to be processed and bottled for the winter, my wife was willing for me to go. As I departed, I noticed her alone in the kitchen with no help from the family. It turned out that all of our teenage helpers had left for a Mutual activity.

"As I drove toward my BYU office, I asked myself: 'What great intellectual achievement will I make tonight that is more important than making grape juice? Even if I do write something fine, will my spending an extra evening on academic work be more important than what is happening at home?' The answer was obvious. I made a U-turn and drove back to the house. When I walked in, my wife said: 'What happened? Did you run out of gas?' 'No,' I said. 'I decided there wasn't anything down there more important than helping you make grape juice.'

"As I rolled up my sleeves and put on an apron, I noticed tears in her eyes. We had a lovely, memorable evening together. Not only did we share work, we visited in-depth and shared some tender moments. As our children arrived home, they were all affected by what was happening. One of them jokingly said, 'My, aren't we domestic tonight,' but there was a serious feeling behind it" ("The Way to Christlike Love," *Ensign,* December 1982, 51). The understanding that can occur when each spouse views the world from the other's lens (and in this case, responds to the increased understanding!) will bond the two and unite their hearts.

Barriers to Listening with Your Heart

Listeners frequently resist listening with their hearts because they are caught up in their own fears. They turn the subject of the conversation to themselves, because they too seek understanding. Frequently, a wife finds it difficult to listen to her husband, or a husband to his wife, because each is feeling overanxious about his or her own agenda. A Latter-day Saint husband and wife who each feels overwhelmed by their various responsibilities may both seek the understanding of the other.

Husband: "I'm so overwhelmed. I've got seventeen people to interview this week."

Wife: "You think you're overwhelmed! I did nothing but drive children to appointments all day long. I haven't even touched the laundry."

Husband: "I don't know how I'm going to fit these appointments in. I have to be out of town Tuesday and Wednesday."

Wife: "Great. Our son has a baseball game Wednesday, and you won't even be there to watch him pitch."

Husband: "We have a ward temple trip planned for Saturday, and if I don't interview some of these people they won't be able to attend the temple."

Wife: "So you're going to be gone Saturday too? I guess that means you're not going to take the boys waterskiing like you promised."

In this conversation the wife hears the words that her husband says but she doesn't consider what's going on in his head as he speaks. Likewise, the husband is so focused on what's happening in his head, he fails to listen to his wife. This phenomenon has been called "negative listening" because it's truly the opposite of listening. Negative listening occurs when the listener is focused only on what he wants to say and is paying little or no attention to what he hears. In this case the wife is concerned about what is on her mind—the children's activities—and the husband is concerned about what he has on his mind—the temple recommend interviews.

Both the husband and wife in the above example are overwhelmed and in need of somebody to listen with understanding. They both want to shed some of the concerns that weigh them down. However, when they are both overanxious about being understood, and both jump in with their own concerns, neither husband nor wife is able to obtain the understanding they crave.

Staying Focused

Husbands and wives who want to understand the burdens a spouse carries can do so with ease if they put themselves in the other's shoes and pay close attention to how it feels over there. Therefore, each spouse will want to take the opportunity to put his or her own feelings aside for a moment and go over and be in his or her partner's space for a while.

Contrast the preceding conversation, where each speaker has his or her own agenda, with the following conversation, where the focus stays on the first speaker.

Husband: "I'm so overwhelmed. I've got seventeen people to interview this week."

Wife: "Seventeen people. Wow! That's a lot!" (She's thinking of his dilemma, not hers.)

Husband: "I don't know how I'm going to fit these appointments in. I have to be out of town Tuesday and Wednesday."

Wife: "Well, today's Monday, so that really only gives you Thursday and Friday to fit them in." (The topic is still on his list of concerns, and hasn't shifted to hers.)

Husband: "Exactly. We have a ward temple trip planned for Saturday, and if I don't interview some of these people they won't be able to attend the temple."

Wife: "I can see it's really important that you find a way for these people to be interviewed before Saturday."

Can you imagine how different the husband feels at the conclusion of this conversation compared to how he feels at the conclusion of the first conversation? In the first case, he probably feels more overwhelmed because the wife has practically doubled his burden. Now he's concerned about the seventeen interviews, plus the ball game and the waterskiing trip. In the second conversation, he still has seventeen interviews, but there are two people concerned about making the interviews happen. He feels the weight spread out over two sets of shoulders, and it feels half as burdensome. Rather than doubling the husband's perceived load, the wife has cut that load in half. When a Church leader feels that someone else comprehends the weight of his or her burden, it significantly lightens the burden. You may even see your spouse sit up straighter and walk with a lighter step because you have lifted some of the burden from his or her shoulders.

Now that the husband feels a bit lighter, it is possible for the wife to bring up some of her own concerns. This time when she brings up her concerns about the car pool and the ballpark, and so on, her husband has space in his head that he can devote to her concerns. He is not completely consumed with his own problems.

Of course, the wife could have been the first to air her concerns in this situation, and the husband could have waited until her concerns were resolved to air his own. The point is, both spouses can't seek understanding simultaneously. One of the couple will need to set his own anxiety aside for a moment and allow the other to express hers.

When you listen with your heart, you will find it irresistible to console your spouse. You will be so in tune with his or her feelings that you will care to an equal degree about the concerns being related to you. The other concerns competing for your attention will not seem more important than the concerns of the one on whom you are focused.

At the conclusion of listening selflessly, your own concerns may even vanish. They may pale in comparison to your spouse's concerns and you may choose not to attend to them. However, if they still exist, it's appropriate to request an opportunity to bring up your own concerns.

My first baby was a preemie, born six weeks early, in Tulsa, Oklahoma, where my husband and I had moved three months earlier. The moment the baby was delivered the doctors whisked him away into a newborn intensive care unit. My husband and I were not permitted to see him or touch him before they took him away. Days passed and I lay in my hospital bed asking questions about my baby: "What's wrong with my baby? Is he okay? Will he live?" The nurses didn't have any answers. The doctors didn't stop by. So I just lay alone in the hospital bed and wept.

The only visitors who stopped by during that lonely hospital stay were the Relief Society presidency of our new ward, and they brought me a corn plant in a three-inch pot.

I carried that corn plant with me through six moves. It grew as my preemie baby grew. I replanted it in a six-inch pot, and then in a ten-inch pot. Eventually it stood waist high.

The first time we moved my husband asked me why I didn't just leave the corn plant behind. We could easily buy another corn plant when we arrived at our new home. It wouldn't survive in the moving van, and certainly I didn't want to take it on a plane. But I wouldn't leave my corn plant. My husband thought I was being ridiculous. The plant was worth only a couple dollars. We could buy a dozen corn plants once we arrived at our new home, he argued. Still, I insisted on bringing my corn plant.

"What is so special about this particular plant?" my husband asked in exasperation as I clutched it to my breast.

"Do you remember when Brandon was born?" I reminded my husband. "I was the saddest I have ever been in my life," I explained. "No one was there for us. We were miles and miles away from home, and it was the sisters of Zion who came to comfort me. This plant reminds me of the love and compassion they showed to us. It is my treasure. I cannot leave it behind."

Bret understood. He listened with his heart, and he felt what I was feeling. The plant has moved with us ever since.

When you listen with your heart you resist the temptation to tell your own story or let your own concerns invade the conversation. You have the ability to fully and selflessly focus on the person sharing the feelings.

Listening without Giving Advice

The ability to listen selflessly can also prevent another common communication error from creeping into your relationship.

Because it is often overwhelming to learn of another's struggles, your first instinct may be to try and end those struggles, to put a stop to them quickly. You may be immediately inclined to respond with a plethora of advice. Your desire to offer advice can frequently be the result of your own discomfort with the overwhelming situation.

Husbands and wives may try *too* hard to be helpful to their overloaded Church leader. You may become so distressed by your loved one's suffering that you are willing to jump in and do something, anything, in order to demonstrate your support.

The task of a supportive spouse is actually far easier than this. A supportive spouse does not need to come up with brilliant solutions to problems. A supportive spouse need only listen carefully enough to comprehend the problem.

The beauty of listening without trying to solve the problem is that your spouse will frequently discover the answers he is looking for in the process of speaking the problem out loud. Because you are a good sounding board, he may be able to solve the problem by himself. He may have had the answer to the problem all along but not known it until he started discussing his feelings of frustration. Because you were a good listener and you tried to be with him and appreciate what he was going through, it helped him see the problem more clearly (even though the exact situation he is dealing with may be confidential and therefore not discussed at all) and come up with his own solution.

A good listener serves much the same function as a personal journal: when you are forced to formulate a thought well enough to put it into words, the thought becomes clearer. Discussing his feelings with a loved one, putting his concern into words another person can comprehend, helps the speaker clarify his thoughts.

In some cases the Church leader you married may want your advice and counsel, and he may beg you for suggestions. However, if the leader is still trying to dissect the problem, and you jump in with a solution to a problem he doesn't yet clearly understand and can't discuss in detail, you will not be offering a service. Should you desire to act as a sounding board to your loved one, you need to take caution not to obstruct his efforts to merely determine the question.

At times I have felt like a grandmother sitting on the edge of the sofa watching *Jeopardy*, with my hand pointing at the television, shouting, "What is . . . Greece?" When someone thinks he knows the answer, it's difficult to stay in his seat. However, the only one who scores any points in this game of answers is the contestant who has been asked the question.

This is a principle my patient husband taught me through years of tutoring.

About Christmastime during Bret's second year as bishop,

sacrament meeting attendance in our ward dropped drastically. Bret came home one Sunday evening heavily discouraged.

"Only sixty-seven people attended sacrament meeting today," he said.

My first inclination was to offer solutions. And I did—in droves. "You need to call these people to repentance," I said. "You need to make honoring the Sabbath the subject of every sacrament meeting for the next year," I exaggerated. "You need to write all these people a letter and remind them of all the Lord has given them and chastise them for being too selfish to give back one day a week."

My discouraged husband didn't say another word. He stared past me to a spot behind me on the wall. The frown on his face deepened and his lips tightened. It was obvious I was not helping.

"What's the matter?" I asked.

"Every time I tell you about a problem I'm having, you always throw out a solution," Bret said, in a voice so soft I had to lean forward to hear. "I know the solutions. I just need to share the problem."

Bret instinctively knew one of the most basic rules of marital communications, the rule I teach virtually every couple that steps into my office. Here I was breaking my own rule! I knew better than to offer unsolicited advice. Unsolicited advice disrupts communication almost every time it's offered.

The Danger of Advice

Offering unsolicited advice inhibits communication between a Church leader and the supportive spouse for several reasons. First of all, it implies that the Church leader can't solve the problem on his own. Second, it implies that the advice giver is so smart that he or she knows all the answers. Neither implication is accurate. No one ever has all the answers. If anyone has answers, the Church leader is more likely to have answers than the spouse, because he or she is intimately acquainted with the problem. The spouse knows only what the leader has shared. In addition, the leader is entitled to personal revelation regarding his or her own stewardship.

Another danger of offering unsolicited advice is that the advice giver may miss the point of the conversation. Often when Church leaders share a problem, they just want someone to commiserate with them. They may know the solution all along. The whole point of starting the conversation is to enlist empathy. A supportive spouse may entirely miss the point if he or she starts offering advice. He may fail to offer empathy altogether.

A supportive spouse who listens without offering suggestions will find that the leader opens up and shares more and more. Such a spouse will find the Church leader more and more grateful for the support and more and more solicitous of the spouse's company. A spouse who says what's on his or her mind every time the Church leader tries to share a burden, rather than trying to truly hear what's on the leader's mind, will find that Church leader increasingly less willing to share his or her emotional concerns.

Sorely repentant, I vowed to respond differently the next time my husband shared his grief about sacrament meeting attendance. Fortunately, Bret was forgiving enough to give me another chance.

"Only sixty-seven people showed up to sacrament meeting again today," the bishop began.

"Wow, that's not very many," I responded.

"Usually we average three times that amount," he added.

"We do?" I asked.

"Yes. I wonder what has been happening lately."

"It could be a number of things." (I refrained from sharing what I thought those things were.)

"Maybe they show up late and miss sacrament meeting," he mused.

"So you think more people arrive by the end of the three-hour block?"

"Yes. I see lots of people in the hall that I didn't see in the chapel."

"That could be it," I said.

"It could also be the holidays—lots of people are out of town." Bret was looking into my eyes this time, not at the spot on the wall.

"Yes."

"It could be people are too busy preparing for the holidays, out shopping and things."

"That would be ironic," I ventured.

"Wouldn't it, though? Here we are, celebrating the birth of the Savior of the world, and instead of honoring him they are scuttling about, forgetting the very reason for the celebration." The bishop was beginning to get some things off his chest.

"It's pretty sad," I responded. I wanted him to continue, so I was careful not to make any suggestions.

"They just don't get it," he said.

"They don't seem to."

"I need to help them understand."

"Do you think you can?"

"That's my job, isn't it? I'm their bishop."

"I guess it is."

"I need to bear my testimony to them. They need to feel the Spirit."

"When you bear your testimony, it sure invites the Spirit."

"I think I'll start doing that next Sunday. I'll do it in sacrament meeting and in the other meetings. Then those who arrive late can hear. If I do it every week for the month of December, most of the active members will have attended one of the four weeks."

"That sure would be in keeping with the spirit of the season," I offered.

The bishop smiled and I didn't know why. "You're wonderful," he said.

"I don't know what's so wonderful about me," I responded. I truly had not offered a single word of wisdom: nothing that sparkled, nothing that made me shine.

"You're a wonderful listener," he said. "Thank you."

"You're a patient teacher," I laughed, remembering that I had not always been such a wonderful listener. "Thank you."

A Time and Place for Advice

The Church leader you support may indeed want your advice on occasion. You will recognize such occasions because the leader will usually ask for your insights. The conversation will begin with, "What do you think about . . . ?" or "I need get your opinion . . ."

If you find it difficult to determine whether your spouse is requesting empathy or is seriously seeking advice, you can simply ask: "Do you want to know what I think?" In a marriage there is nothing wrong with asking your spouse if he or she wants you to simply listen or if he or she actually wants a response. It would be nice if, as soon as you exchanged rings on your wedding day, you developed a magical ability to read each other's minds. Since that kind of magic doesn't exist, only those who ask will know for sure whether they are offering solicited or unsolicited advice.

Once you have done an excellent job listening, and your loved one feels you truly understand the problem, he may indeed seek your advice. Your attentive responses prove that you understand his feelings, so your spouse will consider your opinion more relevant than before. At this point your loved one may relish your perspective.

Open communication between husband and wife will leave no doubt as to when it is appropriate to share one's opinion. Such open communication occurred between Sister Ann S. Reese and her husband. "When my husband was a bishop, he bore his testimony often, as bishops are wont to do. Many times he expressed appreciation for me, and he would say that I was 'the light' of his life. He said it so often that a few of our friends began to tease me good-naturedly about it. I asked him, tactfully, if it wasn't time he found another phrase. He firmly said, 'My dear, you can tell me how to do many things, but do not tell me how to bear my testimony'" ("Being a Wife," *Ensign*, September 1984, 58).

An Eternal Pattern

The Savior set a pattern for giving counsel and direction. Even the Son of Man, who always has the correct answers, frequently chooses to wait to share those answers until the recipient seeks them.

Virtually every section of the Doctrine and Covenants was given in response to the Prophet Joseph's inquiry. The Lord revealed the necessary ordinances for restoring his gospel upon this earth to Joseph when he was ready to receive them. Joseph showed he was ready by inquiring of the Lord.

Throughout the scriptures are examples of prophets who received answers they needed when they were ready and they showed their readiness by asking for the Lord's guidance.

Nephi asked, "Whither shall I go that I may find ore to molten?" (1 Nephi 17:9).

Captain Moroni asked "whither the armies of the Nephites should go to defend themselves against the Lamanites" (Alma 43:23).

The Brother of Jared asked, "Whither shall we steer?" (Ether 2:19).

This principle is also clearly demonstrated in the holy temples.

The Doctrine and Covenants says, "If thou shalt ask, thou shalt receive revelation upon revelation, knowledge upon knowledge, that thou mayest know the mysteries and peaceable things—that which bringeth joy, that which bringeth life eternal" (D&C 42:61).

Even our Heavenly Father, who does have all the correct answers, at times waits until asked to reveal those answers, knowing that the answer won't do the receiver any good unless he or she is receptive and prepared to receive it. Elder Richard G. Scott has taught that "since the Lord will not force you to learn, you must exercise your agency to authorize the Spirit to teach you" ("To Acquire Knowledge and the Strength to Use It Wisely," *Brigham Young University 2000–2001 Speeches* [Provo: Brigham Young University, 2001] 158).

An individual who asks for guidance indicates a readiness and willingness to benefit from guidance.

What a perfect paradigm for those who believe they may have some insights that might bless their loved ones in their Church service. When our loved ones are ready for our insights, they will ask.

CHAPTER 6

BUYING INTO
THE WORK

PRESIDENT GORDON B. HINCKLEY HAS TAUGHT US
that that new converts need three things for their testimonies to
thrive: a friend, a responsibility, and to be nurtured by the word
of God (see "Converts and Young Men," *Ensign,* May 1997, 47).
Consider the value of new members receiving a responsibility or a
calling in the Church. President Thomas S. Monson tells us
responsibility brings "interest, stability, and growth" ("They Will
Come," *Ensign,* May 1997, 44).

If you have served as a leader of youth, you know that an
effective way to assure that your youth attend an activity is to give
them an assignment. Youth are encouraged to plan firesides, find
speakers, plan youth conferences, conduct meetings, and arrange
joint activities. Not only does this help them develop leadership
skills, but it also helps them "buy into" the work—they feel it is
their work too, and they want to make sure it is a success.

This principle, which applies to new members and our youth,
can have relevance to the husband or wife of a devoted Church

leader. A husband who is involved in the same cause as his wife—
or a wife who is involved in the same cause as her husband—will
support the work with his hands as well as his heart.

If your spouse's work is your work too, you will do everything
you can to assure its success. You are both covenant-keeping
Latter-day Saints. You *both* feel strongly about proclaiming the
gospel, perfecting the Saints, and redeeming the dead. As husband
and wife, you are not on opposite teams with competing causes.
You are companions, jointly devoted to the same cause.

Every conversation a husband and wife have about the Lord's
work ought to have a tone of togetherness, an underlying
implication that this is what they both want.

SIDE BY SIDE PHYSICALLY

Husbands can help their wives buy into the work, and wives
can help their husbands buy into the work in a number of ways.
Many a husband has been recruited to hang balloons high above
the gymnasium floor before a New Year's Eve dance. Many a wife
has been invited to bake brownies for a Christmas gift basket.
Lucky couples may even be called to team-teach in Primary or
Sunday school. These opportunities to serve together can provide
a delightful experience for both husband and wife and can occur
with regularity when a husband or wife volunteers to assist a
spouse in a calling.

Finding ways to serve together grows in importance as the
demands of a calling grow. A couple may drift apart when the
busy servant of the Lord plows ahead without considering his or
her spouse. If your spouse does not use you as a resource, remind
your spouse that you are available to assist with some of the activities that consume much of his or her time. As you work together,

your spouse will find that his load seems lighter, and both of you will find that your marriage is stronger.

Visible ways husbands and wives can serve together include

- visiting new members together
- visiting those who are in the hospital
- setting up for socials
- cleaning up after socials
- typing or formatting newsletters
- driving boys to Scout camp
- visiting girls' camp
- chaperoning Church dances
- attending/officiating at weddings
- attending/officiating at funerals
- refereeing/playing/coaching/watching Church ball games
- baby-sitting, moving furniture, or performing similar acts of service

There is no reason Dad has to go one direction on Saturday and Mom another, both serving in the Church but both drifting apart. You may have heard the saying, "Life is sweeter when shared with a friend." Likewise, service is sweeter when shared with a spouse.

Service together doesn't always have to start on your feet. You can serve together by expressing mutual concern about an issue facing your spouse. You can counsel with your spouse as you share your views on a situation.

Elder M. Russell Ballard, while speaking at a general women's meeting in October 1991, said, "Your opinions are valuable, even essential, to the Brethren because no one else has your perspective and insights" ("Be an Example of the Believers," *Ensign*, November 1991, 96).

Let your spouse know that you care about what's important to him and invite your spouse to consider the possibility that in some matters you might be available to share insight or perspective.

CONTRIBUTING IDEAS

Quite frequently, the contribution that a beloved husband or wife makes to help the Church leader succeed in his or her calling is not a physical contribution. You may not always be asked to lend strong hands or a strong back. You may be called upon instead to lend a strong mind.

Husbands and wives of devoted Church leaders may have deep spiritual insights to share. The husband or wife of a devoted Church leader may make sensitive observations based on his or her own realm of experience.

Two seemingly small people in the story of Naaman and Elisha loom very large in my mind. In the story, Naaman's wife is waited upon by a "little maid," an Israelite woman captured in battle. It is this little maid, full of faith, who suggests that Naaman seek to be healed of leprosy by going to see the Israelite prophet. Although a very unlikely source from which to accept influence, the little maid had had experiences Naaman had not. Naaman accepts this possibility and takes the woman's advice.

Later, when Elisha tells Naaman to bathe in the dirty Jordan, he refuses until, once again, a servant respectfully speaks up. "My father, if the prophet had bid thee do some great thing, wouldest thou not have done it?" (see 2 Kings 5:8–14).

Naaman, because he is willing to take counsel from humble sources, benefits immeasurably. These servants know something about humility, and Naaman is willing to learn what they know.

HUMBLE ANSWERS

One of the most frequent admonitions in all of scripture is the Lord's plea that we call on him (see Richard Eyre, *The Discovery of Joy,* rev. ed. [Salt Lake City: Deseret Book, 2000], 93). We are to pray to him over our fields, our flocks, our households, our enemies (see Alma 34:19–22). The Lord wants us to turn to him, the source of all knowledge, with the questions that plague us. If we do, he will provide the answers we seek.

The answers he provides, however, may not come in the miraculous ways we imagine. We might not see angels, have visions, or dream dreams. The answers we seek may not always come directly from the Lord. Our answers may appear in the form of other human beings who cross our paths. Our answers may come when we hear something spoken that rings true. Our answers might come as we read and apply scriptures to the problems we face.

There is no doubt that the Lord will provide answers when we come to him with questions. We, however, must be humble enough to recognize the answers in whatever form they are sent.

The scriptures are the surest source to tap when we need answers to life's problems. If we want answers to life's questions, the most comprehensive encyclopedia on earth is the scriptures. When we read the scriptures, passages we have read before come to have new meaning in light of our current questions.

At times, scriptural answers may not always come directly from the books themselves. Scriptural answers will also come from people who study the scriptures and understand eternal principles. Prophets and Apostles testify of scriptural truths. The Lord places people in our lives who can share the wisdom and insight they have gained from reading and pondering the scriptures.

Two seminary teachers were driving some distance to a training meeting, when one of them, Sister Call, confided in her passenger. "The whole reason I'm coming tonight is to talk to our high councilor," she said. "I need to ask him some questions the students raised that I don't have answers for." After the meeting Sister Call pulled her high councilor aside. For a long time they discussed the questions that plagued Sister Call. The high councilor didn't have the specific answers she sought, but he encouraged her to continue pondering and praying for answers. On the way home Sister Call couldn't help but think, I came all this way tonight specifically to talk with the high councilor, and I'm going home as confused as before. In the course of the drive, Sister Call shared her gospel questions with her traveling companion, who, as a fellow seminary teacher, had recently studied the very topic that confused Sister Call. The traveling companion provided the needed answers to the questions that had plagued Sister Call for weeks—answers Sister Call had never expected to glean from such a humble source.

Of all the people the Lord might place in a Church leader's path to provide answers to questions, the spouse is a very logical person. A spouse intimately understands the concerns of the Lord's servant, cares to an infinite degree, and ponders and prays for answers for the Church leader as much as or more than anybody else. We know the Lord will send angels to lift us up in times of trial. A spouse can be one of those very angels the Lord has promised to send to lift the burden of a dedicated Church servant.

BEWARE OF PRIDE

It takes a great deal of humility to ask others for wisdom and advice. A Church servant may begin serving in a calling with the idea that he or she should be able to fulfill the calling based entirely on his own inspiration, wisdom, and insight. In reality, there are people all around who can keep a leader from reinventing the wheel.

A very humbling experience taught me to listen to those who counseled me in my calling. Once I was asked to direct a road show in Tulsa, Oklahoma. A talented musician in the ward wrote all the songs for the show. She wrote original music and words and even created one song in the form of a round, so the two groups sang different lyrics but the music blended perfectly. She wrote one of the most clever, original road shows I have ever seen.

After several weeks of working on the show, the youth could perform it perfectly. They knew their lines; they knew the lyrics. The costumes were sewn and the set painted. The night of the road shows we all reported to a local high school, where we would perform on the stage of the huge auditorium.

The stage was so large that most of the wards performed their road shows in front of the curtain. The musician who wrote our road show suggested that we perform in front of the curtain as well. However, I thought our ward was bigger, better, louder, and more colorful than all the other wards. I determined that we could perform on the real stage and pull off a superior performance.

The result was disastrous. The stage was so large and the auditorium so massive that our little cast was swallowed up in the space on the stage. Few people could even hear the clever lyrics of the songs the youth had polished to perfection. Twenty years later I still regret that I was too proud to listen to the advice of those who knew more about theater than I did.

Pride may keep individuals from considering others' advice simply because they may not seem qualified enough or important enough to do so. This very problem plagued the people of Nazareth, where the Savior grew up. The Savior of the world taught in the synagogue in Nazareth, and his neighbors discounted him, asking, "Is not this Joseph's son?" Christ then testified, "No prophet is accepted in his own country" (see Luke 4:16–24).

In answer to prayer, Heavenly Father may encourage leaders to glean truths from available resources (as humble as those resources may seem) and then take those answers to him for confirmation that they are his will. In a sense he wants the leader to "do the homework."

Homework includes reading the scriptures, studying the topic, and quizzing those mortals with wisdom and experience, as well as praying for inspiration. Doctrine and Covenants section 9 helps us understand the process:

"Behold, you have not understood; you have supposed that I would give it unto you, when you took no thought save it was to ask me.

"But, behold, I say unto you, that you must study it out in your mind; then you must ask me if it be right, and if it is right I will cause that your bosom shall burn within you; therefore, you shall feel that it is right.

"But if it be not right you shall have no such feelings, but you shall have a stupor of thought that shall cause you to forget the thing which is wrong; therefore, you cannot write that which is sacred save it be given you from me" (vv. 7–9).

During the homework stage, leaders can glean many answers from mere mortals. Brethren or sisters who have served in callings previously can provide insight. They inevitably pick up a tidbit here and there from their tenure in a calling that they probably would be delighted to pass along to the next person who fills the calling. Church leaders can learn from the expertise of those who have gone before, be they musicians with expertise in theater or seminary teachers who extensively study the gospel. Husbands and wives are some of the most obvious resources available—but somewhat like a prophet not being recognized in his own hometown, these resources often go untapped.

The effort put forth in the homework stage of getting answers leads to tremendous learning and growth; it helps us appreciate the answers we find because we have worked for them and thus increased the chances that we will act on what we have learned. In addition, when a beloved companion joins in the quest for answers, the process of the couple growing together blesses the marriage in a deep and poignant way.

As the spouse of a devoted Church servant, you probably don't consider yourself the fountain of all knowledge. However, you undoubtedly possess some areas of expertise. The Lord may choose to answer his servant's prayers through you.

In the end, if your spouse chooses to turn to you for wisdom and insight, it does not mean he will always take your advice. It means he is doing his homework. He will make the ultimate decision as he considers your advice along with everything else he knows, including facts you are not privy to. Ultimately, it is Heavenly Father who will confirm that the decisions he makes are correct.

The Church leader who takes advantage of the insights a devoted husband or wife can share will realize numerous blessings.

The individual with the official calling gains perspective and insight. The marriage partner gains commitment to the work of the Lord. The marriage grows in unity and love.

The devoted Church leader in your home may not recognize right away the value of a loyal resource in the form of a husband or wife. Church leaders may assume they must rely entirely on inspiration from the Holy Ghost for every decision. To gain insights from a mortal may seem an unfair advantage—like skiing on parabolic skis compared to the old straight and narrow skis; the new skis make skiing so easy it almost feels like cheating.

This assumption reminds me of my own attitude as a student of competitive speech. Once I was competing in a forensics meet and was enrolled in two events in the same meet, extemporaneous speaking and impromptu speaking. In the extemporaneous speaking rounds we were given access to such magazines as *Time, U.S. News and World Report,* and *Newsweek,* and we were given thirty minutes to prepare a five-minute talk. In the impromptu speaking rounds we were given no materials, and we had only one minute to prepare a talk.

As luck would have it, when I entered an impromptu speaking round, one of the topics I could choose to speak about was the exact topic I had just spoken on in the previous extemporaneous speaking round. I had just finished reading several magazine articles on this precise topic. I had statistics at my fingertips and quotes from experts fresh in my mind. If I chose to speak on that same topic again, I could give a far better speech than a speech that relied on my impressions or my memory. It was too good to be true. In fact, it was so fortuitous, I felt like it was cheating to speak on the same topic, so I chose a different topic.

Back then I was suspicious of situations that were "too good to be true." Now I recognize that the Lord loves us and wants to bless our lives; and a serendipitous resource discovered in our own homes may very well be the way he chooses to answer our prayers.

THE RESOURCEFUL SWEETHEART

Wives may possess a number of talents that will help their husbands fulfill their callings, and husbands may possess a number of talents that help their wives fulfill their callings. Wives may excel at money management, finding a job, writing a resume, or investing. They may understand child care, organizing a home, or frugal meal planning. They may have talents for teaching, working with computers, upholstering, or any number of other talents they can share with needy members. Wives may understand, in general, the personal struggles of the women in the ward more readily than the priesthood leaders do.

Husbands may possess a number of talents that will help their wives fulfill their callings. Husbands can help fix broken pipes, diagnose vehicle breakdowns, or offer a strong back. Husbands may have experience working in organizations and understand the personality dynamics of leadership. Husbands may be recruited to offer blessings or take fatherless boys on campouts, even if it's the wife's responsibility to care for a particular family.

Recall from an earlier chapter the ninety-eight-year-old brother with the fungus who came to stay at our home while his wife went to a wedding. Let me tell you the rest of the story. I was the wife's visiting teacher. I was the one who invited the elderly gentleman to come stay at our home so she could attend her granddaughter's wedding. I didn't anticipate that this dear brother might not want a tiny little woman, who was not his wife, helping him to the bathroom throughout the night. Although it was I who volunteered for this act of service, it was my husband who awoke every two hours in the middle of the night and rubbed medicine on the painful rash. I apologized over and over to my husband for my getting him into the situation. I acknowledged that I had taken on a commitment to serve and that he had, of necessity, come to my rescue. My husband never complained about his service. He never chastised me for my lack of foresight.

He served with a loving heart and tender, caring hands. He rendered service I simply could not render myself.

You may be in a position to serve when your spouse can't. Your spouse may be in a position to serve when you can't. You can complement one another when you both see yourselves as players on the same team, working together to further the kingdom of God on this earth.

While keeping in mind the cautions revealed in the previous chapter about offering advice, recognize that you may contain a rich strain of wisdom or insight should your loved one choose to tap that resource.

A BLESSING FOR YOU PERSONALLY

Recall the lesson from the beginning of this chapter: youth participate more enthusiastically in activities they have been invited to help plan. Recall also President Hinckley's counsel that if new converts are to stay active, they need a responsibility.

The same principle holds true in a marriage. When your loved one receives an assignment and you become involved, you will be more interested in the success of the assignment than if you are not involved. This is because his work is your work too. Both husband and wife desire the same goals. You are on the same team. You are pulling the same cart in the same direction.

Once when my husband served as a bishop he became concerned about a young woman in the ward who was not keeping the Church's dress standards. Tamara liked to advertise her very thin, long legs by wearing extremely short skirts. At the bishop's request, I began a dialogue with Tamara.

"Can I have all your old skirts when you go to BYU? I'm short enough they will reach my knees!" I joked. When Tamara continued to purchase new skirts at the clothing shop where she worked, I continued my good-natured teasing.

"Oh, I see you bought me another skirt. I'm going to get a whole new wardrobe when you go to school." Tamara didn't throw away all her short skirts at once, but she did stop buying new ones.

Late one Saturday night, the bishop and I were sound asleep when the telephone rang. I sleepily answered it and nudged my husband. "It's Tamara. She sounds kind of upset."

As the bishop dragged himself out of bed into the privacy of his study, I lay in bed marveling. I didn't even consider the intrusion into our much-needed sleep. Instead, I felt only concern for Tamara. Tamara was one of my sheep too. I had invested a little of my own heart in Tamara's salvation, and I was grateful that a righteous husband was doing his own part to help Tamara find her way home to our Heavenly Father.

Regardless of whether they are working on the same assignment, or on different assignments in the same vineyard, when a husband and a wife work together in the Lord's vineyard they both rejoice when any of the trees bear fruit and both are willing to make sacrifices for this to happen.

When both a husband and a wife use their individual talents to serve the Lord, they do not receive *vicarious* joy when the other succeeds. They receive *literal* joy. The success that occurred is a personal success. They are both players on the same team. Like tennis partners in a doubles match, when one partner hits a winner, they both win.

A young bishop was faced with the following situation: a particular sister in the ward liked to speak at the podium every single fast Sunday, but her comments strayed a little beyond those appropriate for a testimony. As soon as fast meeting was open for testimonies, she would jump up and race to the podium in order to begin her testimony before anyone else stood. She spoke at length about her most recent visit to the hospital and the illnesses she feared she possessed. She told the congregation about her children, who had not been to visit in ever so long, and about the new elderly care facility she was trying to get into but for which she was still on the waiting list. Once in a while her comments included her testimony of the gospel. But even then the testimony was intertwined with the life and times of her doctors and the assisted-living staff.

The bishop spoke kindly with the elderly sister about appropriate testimonies, but the health updates continued. In exasperation one fast Sunday the bishop asked his wife what more he could do without hurting the sister's feelings. The bishop's wife suggested they conduct an experiment. It was obvious the sister wanted everybody to know all about her ailments, so the bishop's wife suggested they give the sister a chance to talk about herself before testimony meeting. The bishop's wife volunteered to be the first one to test their experiment. Before fast and testimony meeting she stopped the sister in the hall.

"Did you receive the results back from your blood test?" she asked.

The elderly sister responded at length about her iron levels and her cholesterol.

"Have you had any luck getting into Cypress Village?"

The bishop's wife learned all about the long waiting list, and the chances that a spot would open up soon.

"How are your daughters down south?" the bishop's wife asked.

The sister tried to give her daughters the benefit of the doubt, acknowledging how busy their lives had become and how difficult it was to travel with small children.

Truly it was an enlightening conversation, and the bishop's wife began to care about the details of the sister's life. In fact, she felt remorseful that she hadn't asked on her own, without being motivated by duty. The elderly sister obviously needed a friend in the Church. She needed someone to care about her personally. The reason the sister shared her life's story with the whole congregation was that she didn't have anyone else to share it with.

Late that evening, at end of the fast day, the bishop and his wife fell exhausted into bed. The bishop was almost asleep when he rolled over. "Was our favorite sister at church today?" he asked.

"Uh-huh," his wife sleepily affirmed.

"She didn't bear her testimony," he remarked with wonder.

"Nope." The bishop's wife was too tired to tell him what happened.

"Did you talk to her?" He wouldn't relent.

"Uh-huh."

"It worked!" he exclaimed.

"Uh-huh."

"You're a genius. I'll take next month," he offered.

"It's okay. I'll do it." The bishop's wife wasn't as sleepy anymore. "She's truly a wonderful sister. She needs a friend. I want to know how she's doing. I'll keep you updated."

CHAPTER 7

∽

LIGHTEN THE
LEADER'S LOAD

THINK OF ALL THE TIMES A CHILD HAS APPROACHED
you for help while you were in the middle of an important task.
"Mom, can you come push me on the swing?" "Dad, can you
drive me to my friend's house?" In order to assist your child, you
have to put your own work aside. Perhaps you have dealt with the
situation like many seasoned parents. You encourage your child
to help you finish your project so you're free to go play with the
child. "Here, pick up a towel and dry these dishes, and then we
can go." "Sit down here beside me and help me fold this basket
of clothes, and then we can go."

A busy Church servant is a lot like a parent involved in an
important task, and in some ways a spouse may be likened to the
child who needs attention. The Church leader can more easily
attend to your request as a spouse when you offer to lift the load
he or she currently carries. Can you imagine how delighted your
spouse would feel if, before asking something of him or her, you
offered to lift a burden? "Can I help you print those flyers so we

can go out tonight?" will help the busy Church servant feel less burdened, whereas, "Can't you hurry up and finish so we can go out?" would add to the burden.

LIGHTEN YOUR PARTNER'S LOAD

Too often a person with a heavy Church calling feels caught in a tug-of-war between family and Church. Church members pull aggressively on one arm, and family members relentlessly cling to the other arm. The poor servant feels as if she is being torn in two. Ideally, the partner of the devoted Church servant will learn not to place competing demands on the Church servant but will try to reduce the demands. Reducing the demands doubles the blessings. First, your sweetheart is done with the task earlier and has time for you. Second, you get to enjoy each other's companionship as you work together to fulfill the tasks that seemed to stand in the way of your togetherness.

Some time ago a woman brought her daughter into my office because the teenage girl showed definite signs of depression. The family had recently adopted three children from a foreign country, increasing the number of children in the family from four to seven. The daughter revealed that she felt completely abandoned and neglected by her mother. Mom had absolutely no time for her anymore. The plan we devised to mend the relationship between this daughter and her mother paralleled the solution that works for busy Church servants and their families. I suggested that this daughter become her mom's "right-hand man." Together they could walk the adopted children in their strollers. Together they could push the adopted children on the swings at the park. This way Mom and Daughter grew closer, and the daughter was able to be a big part of her mom's life. Mom and Daughter felt they were on the same team, as opposed to Mom feeling she was in the middle of a tug-of-war.

Working together can bring as much satisfaction as playing together—or even more. Think of friends you have made over the years. Whom are you close to—those you have served with in various Church callings, or those you join for a weekly game of golf or tennis? Serving together can build relationships at least as effectively as playing together. When you crave time with your devoted loved one, you might consider conjuring up a way to work together even before you conjure up a way to play together.

Ironically, the opposite sometimes occurs when a person becomes steeped in Church service. The spouse may feel as if she's in competition with all those who call upon the Church leader for attention. The spouse may then find more and more tasks that "absolutely must" be performed at home.

A partner who adds demands so that the busy Church servant will spend more time at home will probably win the battle. The busy Church servant will likely cave in and meet those demands. However, in winning this battle the spouse will not win the war. The demands of the calling will remain and may become compounded by negligence. In addition, the couple will miss out on the blessings that can occur as they serve the Lord in unity.

The spouse of a heavily involved Church leader will successfully solicit more "couple time" when, instead of seizing that time, he or she helps lighten the partner's load. Whatever you can do to lighten the load your spouse carries at church will enable him or her to comfortably spend more time on the home front. Then your spouse's decision to come home will be made out of choice, not out of coercion.

A spouse can assume a surprising number of the responsibilities placed upon the servant of the Lord. Church leaders receive all kinds of telephone calls that they need not return personally. Some of those calls can be answered by a spouse. The spouse can field calls for

- telephone numbers of new members
- directions to the church/stake center/bishop's storehouse
- location of ward boundaries
- names and phone numbers of auxiliary leaders
- telephone numbers of leaders from other wards
- dates and times of Church activities
- the names of someone's visiting teachers or home teachers

A Church leader's spouse can easily provide phone numbers, dates, directions, and names of home teachers. Elders quorum presidents and high priest group leaders can keep an updated list of home teaching routes for their wives' use. A map of the ward boundaries will help a spouse determine which ward boundaries callers live within. A list of the bishops from nearby wards will help a spouse know where to refer some of the calls. Of course, a list of organization presidents, compassionate service directors, and so on will help a spouse make appropriate referrals too.

People moving into the area frequently want information on available housing or schools. Their questions may be as diverse as a request for a good mechanic or the days the temple is open. The person who answers the phone can field these phone calls, relieving the Church leader of the responsibility.

The Church leader will appreciate being informed of these calls so if follow-up is required he or she can be familiar with the situation. But a spouse can save a great deal of effort by fielding initial phone calls. By fielding phone calls, you give a gift money can't buy: a great big chunk of time.

You've probably recognized already that when you lighten your spouse's load, your own load increases in weight. Rest assured that we will spend several chapters discussing ways to lighten *your* load. The ultimate goal is to find a way for both you and your sweetheart to spend more time with one another. For the moment, let's look at ways to free up some time for your busy partner.

DO WHAT ONLY YOU CAN DO

While you are chipping in to help lighten your spouse's load, your spouse may be able to shed some of his or her responsibilities too. As busy Church servants choose what they will include on their "to do" lists and what they will not, one very important question is paramount: Am I the only one who can do this task, or can someone else possibly do this task?

There are duties in the Church that only a bishop can do. Only a bishop can interview someone for his or her first temple recommend. Only a bishop can hear the confession of someone caught up in a moral sin. These are responsibilities within the calling that cannot be delegated.

Some personal obligations cannot be delegated. Only you can exercise your body (although it would be a popular invention to find a way for someone else to do our exercises for us). Only Dad can be the real "daddy" on a daughter's daddy-daughter date. Only Dad can be the real father at the fathers and sons outing. Only you can be your spouse's mate.

Once a person with a time-consuming calling distinguishes the responsibilities that can be delegated from those that can't, the leader has the opportunity to make other arrangements for the responsibilities that are not exclusively his.

A Time for Delegation

Whatever the Church leader's highly demanding calling, his load will be lighter if he is willing to separate the aspects of the calling that can be delegated from those that can't.

Devoted Church servants may be reluctant to delegate leadership responsibilities for the following reasons:

- the person they delegate a task to might be overwhelmed by the difficulty of the task
- the person they delegate the task to might not do a good job
- the person they delegate the task to might say no to the assignment
- the person they delegate might say yes and fail to perform the task anyway

All these fears are legitimate, and some might come true. Perhaps few people could do the job as well as you or your spouse does the job. Chances are, the people your spouse delegates to will indeed struggle with the magnitude of the responsibility. These are chances that are worth taking. Members of the Church who struggle to complete difficult assignments inevitably grow as a result. They develop leadership skills that will enable them to take over when your spouse is released!

The principle of delegation will benefit both the leader whose load is lifted and the member who has the opportunity to serve.

In our ward we went through a period where we really lacked leadership. We had a lot of members, but because we live in a military ward, the majority of the priesthood holders were out to sea, and a slew of strong families moved out of the ward all at once. My dear husband tried to fulfill all the responsibilities himself but was physically unable. I realize the Lord will strengthen our backs to enable us to carry even the heaviest load. However, when we are carrying as much as we possibly can, the answer the Lord provides may not be to strengthen our backs; it may be to send in some additional backs.

When our ward lost so much leadership in so short a time, Bret called some very unlikely people to fulfill positions. Many rose to the occasion and grew rapidly, continuing to serve in responsible positions even after our ward regained some leaders. These folks would not have had the opportunity were it not for the tremendous need. Even those of other faiths came to our aid. A chef at a local restaurant came to cook for a ward party and became very friendly with several of the ward members. Another nonmember did a fantastic job with the Cub Scouts.

The Pareto Principle

One of my Presbyterian friends once told me that it is a well-known fact in her church that 20 percent of the members do 80 percent of the work. I smugly thought to myself, *Not in my church. We distribute the work among all the members. Everyone has a calling, so no one group is overburdened with work.* However, in my more humble moments I had to admit that sometimes our statistics don't look a lot different from hers. The 80–20 rule, also called the Pareto Principle, was postulated by Vilfredo Pareto, a nineteenth-century economist. It states that a small number of causes are responsible for a large number of effects. When applied to church service, it often holds true that 20 percent of the people do 80 percent of the work. Although that's not the way The Church of Jesus Christ of Latter-day Saints is set up, we sometimes find a few serving the many.

The percentages of those who serve and those who don't might not be precisely 20 percent and 80 percent in your ward.

The statistics will differ in every ward throughout the Church. The important question is, do we live in wards where a minority of the members do the lion's share of the work?

In my friend's church her pastor makes all the hospital visits himself, counsels all the struggling families, and attends to all welfare needs. Our church is designed differently than my friend's. In a lay ministry we all pitch in and care for one another: home teachers and visiting teachers visit the sick and aid with welfare needs. Our church is designed so that everybody can help in their own way and contribute to the success of the ward, stake, and the Church. The home teaching and visiting teaching programs are ideal vehicles for delegating the care of the flock. They work on a principle similar to a marriage: when your spouse is sick, you take care of your spouse; when you are sick, your spouse takes care of you. If one of you is always sick, and the other one is always doing the care-taking, the caretaker can become extremely overwhelmed with the burden. Likewise, if 80 percent of the ward is always sick (physically, spiritually, or emotionally) and 20 percent of the ward is always taking care of the sick, it can be extremely overwhelming for the 20 percent who are well.

Asking for Help

Delegation may feel like a fancy word for "asking for help," and some people may feel it is a sign of weakness of character to admit that they can't fulfill their callings without a little help.

Asking for help is not a sign of weakness of character. Asking for help is more often a sign of strength of character. A humble man is willing to admit his limitations. There is no shame in asking for help when you have served to your capacity, or when you need to be buoyed up.

Moses was humble enough to admit he needed help because

he was slow of speech. He received it when the Lord provided Aaron as a spokesman. Joseph Smith recognized he could not translate without a scribe, and the Lord provided Oliver Cowdery. Adam needed help, and the Lord provided a helpmeet, Eve. Asking for help when making an effort to serve the Lord should never cause a leader embarrassment or shame.

Even Jesus asked for help. He asked for help when he began his ministry as he called fishermen to leave their nets and learn to preach the gospel. He sent them to heal the sick rather than go himself. At first they could not perform the miracles as well as the Savior. He had to train them. But he still delegated and gave them an opportunity to fail, to learn, and to grow (see Matthew 17:14–21).

The Savior of mankind also asked for help in his hour of greatest need. It appears that he entered the Garden of Gethsemane aware that the task he faced would require a great reservoir of strength. He turned to his beloved Apostles, Peter, James, and John, and said, "My soul is exceeding sorrowful, even unto death: tarry ye here, and watch with me." Apparently he was very serious about his desire for their companionship because he came to them again: "And he cometh unto the disciples, and findeth them asleep, and saith unto Peter, What, could ye not watch with me one hour?" (Matthew 26:38, 40). So great was his anguish, and so overwhelming the task of facing it alone, that he turned to his disciples yet a third time for support.

What a high compliment he paid to his disciples! Although a god, he was willing to turn to these mortals and say, in effect, "I could sure use some help here." With that invitation is the unspoken corollary, "I have a high enough regard for you that I am willing to let you help me." This was a tremendous opportunity for Peter, James, and John. What a great honor it was that the Savior of the world considered them a resource.

In the end, the Apostles did not stay awake to "watch with [him] one hour" (v. 40). His solo suffering was part of the divine plan; ultimately, he took our sins upon himself alone. However, it is a powerful lesson for us to note that in his hour of greatest need, the Savior asked for help. It seems evident that it is not weakness to call upon others in our hour of need. Perhaps his plea was for their benefit, maybe for his own, perhaps for both. Perhaps the recorded verses are for us. They provide a tender and humble example to each of us. What a divine virtue it is to trust others enough to give them an opportunity to come to our aid. Although Peter, James, and John did not have the capacity to watch with the Savior on this transcendent occasion, the Savior still extended the invitation (see Matthew 26:37–40).

You may be one, like me, who wants to raise her hand and shout, "Call on me! I'll stay awake! You can depend on me in your hour of need!" Of course that is not the request our Savior has made of us. But he has made other requests for us to assist him. Each one of us can fight the fatigue that descends upon us when we are weary from our labors, and we can strive to stay awake as we come to the Savior's aid in our own lifetimes.

If you really must fulfill a task alone, the Lord will strengthen your back and provide you with the capacity to fulfill the tasks he has assigned you. However, there will certainly be times that you are not supposed to fulfill the task by yourself. I believe that the Lord knows you are awake. He knows your hand is being raised, eager to come to his aid. However, others may need the opportunity to come to the aid of the Savior. They can do this when you—or your spouse—invite them to assist you in the Lord's work. When you feel unable to complete a task alone, and you have importuned the Lord for strength beyond your capacity, the rescue you receive may be in the form of other individuals.

People who think they are indispensable or that they can do everything themselves without delegating will discover otherwise when in a pinch. Perhaps your spouse needs a little pinch to remind him he's a mere mortal!

If Not Me, Who?

I'm embarrassed to admit that my children used to leave their belongings all over the floor of our house. I found myself running around the house picking up socks, putting away shoes, and hanging up towels and backpacks all day long. I felt as if I worked in the dressing room at Lafayette Galleries, people throwing skirts at my feet and scarves over my head, my arms laden with gowns and my fingers dripping with accessories.

I've never aspired to work in a dressing room at a fashion show, and picking up my children's clothing all day long was not my idea of fun. To remedy this situation I suggested to my children that they ask themselves the question, "If not me, who?"

"How do you expect your shoes to be removed from the family room floor?" I asked my middle son.

"They'll walk away by themselves?" said the child who always knows how to lighten the tone of a conversation.

"Do you think you could tell those shoes when it's time to walk away next time?" I asked him.

It took four children to teach me that the reason they left their belongings all over the house was because a little elf would always come along, perfectly willing and able to pick them up. The little elf was me! Once the little elf stopped magically picking up after my children, they miraculously learned to pick up after themselves.

Members of the Church who seem unwilling to help may be like my children. They are perfectly capable of helping, but why interfere when you or your spouse is already doing such a good job? They may not know how much you need their help until they see how difficult it is for you to serve without them.

One of our family's favorite quotations is a fairly famous saying, "If not me, who? If not now, when?" With maturity our children began to realize that if they didn't pick up after themselves or do their chores, someone else would have to. Fortunately, they have enough compassion for their mom not to burden her with all her chores and all theirs too.

HELP ON THE HOME FRONT

Some of the most overwhelming times for a Church leader are the moments when he realizes his responsibilities at home are slipping through the cracks.

My family belongs to a homeowners' association that is very persnickety about the appearance of the yards in our neighborhood. For many years my dear husband kept an immaculate lawn. He edged, trimmed, and cut the grass, weeded the beds and pruned the bushes conscientiously. Upon receiving a call to serve as a bishop, try as he might, Bret couldn't find an evening or a Saturday to work in the yard. The reality of the situation finally clicked when he received a letter from our homeowners' association. The neighbors had complained because our lawn was so long they feared they would lose their children and small animals in it. They wondered if we could please attend to our yard. Instantly Bret realized that he needed to find a way to relieve himself of some of his responsibilities at home.

Those of you with plentiful resources may chose to hire professionals to help with some of the responsibilities around the house. We decided it was time to teach our three sons how to care for the yard. In another similar situation, a Young Men president was blessed by the services of an appreciative deacon who wanted to show his gratitude to his Young Men president by helping him in the yard.

Youth, I have observed, are frequently willing to provide tender and caring service, not simply to the down and out, but often to their capable leaders.

A couple of young women offered to baby-sit for their Young Women president on the weekends so she could have a date with her husband. With all the time she spent at weekly Young Women activities, presidency meetings, girls' camp, youth conference, youth dances, standards nights, New Beginnings programs, firesides, and young womanhood recognition award ceremonies, she barely had time for her husband. These darling young women recognized an opportunity to be of service to someone not usually considered a candidate for service: those who render service themselves.

Another young woman brought baked goods to the bishopric on the Sundays she knew they would be working at the church past lunchtime. In another ward a computer whiz volunteered to set up a new computer for a busy Church leader.

For the most part, when our youth render service, they will concentrate on the needy. If, on occasion, youth choose to show their gratitude to their leaders by rendering service, leaders can graciously and gratefully accept this expression of love.

The Savior set a beautiful example for us when he allowed others to serve him. He borrowed beds to sleep in; he borrowed boats to sail in; he allowed others to prepare his meals and wash his feet. Ultimately he was laid to rest in a borrowed tomb. It is an honor to serve those who are anxiously engaged in fulfilling the responsibilities the Lord has assigned to them.

When ward members perceive that the leaders they depend on also depend on them, they may feel honored at the opportunity to make a difference. Ideally, when ward members recognize a Church leader is overloaded they will fulfill their own callings with greater zeal in order to lighten that load.

Giving Up Something Good

Sacrifice is often defined as "giving up something good for something better." Some of the things a Church leader finds he does not have time for may be tasks he thoroughly enjoys. Bret used to coach our sons' Pop Warner football teams. He used to run marathons. He used to keep an immaculate lawn. Once he was called as a bishop, there was no way he could continue doing all the things he used to do. Accepting this fact is harder than it sounds.

When you receive a calling, you receive it virtually all at once. One day the bishop or stake president calls you into his office and extends a calling. The next Sunday you are sustained and set apart, and Voilà! You have a line of people waiting to meet with you! Although the calling comes suddenly, changing your lifestyle to adapt to your new calling may not come so suddenly. Bret found he still wanted to coach the kids' football teams and run marathons and keep an immaculate lawn. But there simply weren't enough hours in the day to complete all the things that had previously filled his days plus all the new tasks that came with his calling. A quart jar holds only one quart. If you pour more than one quart of liquid in the jar, some of the liquid will spill out.

When you have given your all, the Lord will give you strength beyond your capacity. I believe this phenomenon is the same thing as grace. The Lord will enable you to reach your goals after all you can do. However, "works" is also a vital part of the "grace and works" equation. Before you ask the Lord to give you strength beyond your own capacity, I believe you need to do what you can do to lighten your own load.

The shock of giving up part of your life B.C. (before calling) won't knock you entirely unconscious if you anticipate some life changes and address these changes individually. A newly appointed Church servant can always wait for a nervous breakdown to convince him he is trying to do too much at once. A newly appointed Church servant could wait until a bunch of people grow really, really angry because he made promises he can't possibly keep. Or a newly called Church servant can design his or her life a little differently.

Choose What to Give Up

You may want to sit down with your leader-spouse and decide what you two can possibly give up from your past life that used to keep you anxiously engaged. As you decide what you will give up and what you will keep, try to give up those things that someone else can do and keep those things that only you can do. In our case, it became apparent that other people could coach football. Other people could cut, edge, and trim the lawn. Bret needed to concentrate on the tasks that he alone could fulfill.

You and your spouse may find it difficult to give up all the roles you used to assume in the past. I know a man who used to stay after every ward social to help clean up and put away tables and chairs. He had a difficult time leaving an event before the door was locked, even if it wasn't his assignment. When he was called to serve in a demanding leadership position, it became necessary to allow others to clean and lock up. Vacuuming the carpet is not something only one person can do.

I've frequently fantasized about life during the Millennium. In a world full of righteous people, where 100 percent of the people fulfill their callings, a bishop, an elders quorum president, or a Relief Society president would have very little to do. They would feel like the Maytag repairman. They'd sit around waiting for a crisis, and it would rarely come.

PART TWO

TAKING CARE
OF YOURSELF

◌

CHAPTER 8

THE CONTRACT: TAKING TIME FOR EACH OTHER

THE WORLD TELLS US THAT ONE PARENT CAN RAISE a child just as effectively as two parents. The world tells us that quality time with our children is just as valuable as quantity time. However, the prophets tell us that the greatest work we will do will be within the walls of our own homes (see Harold B. Lee, "Follow the Leadership of the Church," *Ensign,* July 1973, 98). The prophets believe that "no other success can compensate for failure in the home" (David O. McKay, quoting J. E. McCulloch, *Home: The Savior of Civilization* [Washington, D.C.: The Southern Cooperative League, 1924], 42; in Conference Report, April 1935, 116).

Valiant Latter-day Saints know the prophets speak the truth. Knowing that nothing can substitute for spending time with the family, a Church leader may experience conflict when trying to fulfill a busy Church calling and still spend time with the family.

Our family's dilemma over how to balance family with competing demands rose to a critical level many years ago. I was serving as public communications director for the Church in our area.

My husband watched me dive into the public relations calling wholeheartedly, barely pausing to come up for air. One year I was responsible for a National Family Week program in our area. Our kitchen turned into a photo lab as I edited a promotional video. The dining room table overflowed with stacks of papers in various stages of collation. I spent weeks doing nothing but typing press releases and talking on the telephone. Part of the effort included creating a public service commercial to advertise the "Family of the Year" program.

The day we were to shoot the commercial, I pulled up in front of the police station downtown in my "mom-mobile," the venerable minivan. I planned to run quickly inside and flag down the police officer who was talent for the ad, so I kept my minivan running and ignored the No Parking sign. In my haste to stay on schedule, I locked my keys in the mom-mobile. That wouldn't have been so bad, except my nine-month-old baby was inside, asleep in his car seat. During the forty-five minutes it took for the police to try (unsuccessfully—can you believe it?) to break into the car, and for us to eventually call a locksmith, my son awoke and his screams rose to a forte.

Not only did I hear sarcastic comments from every policeman who walked by (and there were plenty—I was parked, after all, in front of the police station), but later my husband had a few direct and pointed comments to make about the amount of attention and energy I was expending on my calling, at the expense of my family.

Eventually I was released from my public communications calling, and I decided to go to graduate school. You can imagine Bret's reaction when I brought up the subject of graduate school.

His adrenaline started pumping and Danger signs flashed before his eyes. He foresaw me charging ahead with my schooling just as I did with my Church callings. He foresaw late nights with Mom studying in the library and weekend study groups infringing on our family life.

With great foresight, and having learned from experience, Bret reined in my enthusiasm for this new venture before the horses were galloping wildly ahead with the stagecoach broken down on the side of the highway. He agreed to support me in graduate school, under certain conditions, and the conditions would be spelled out in the form of a contract.

THE CONTRACT

Gasp! A contract? Between husband and wife? You might think such formality should be unnecessary among honest, trustworthy adults. Quite the opposite: contracts are what make us honest, trustworthy adults.

You can't get married without a contract. Without a marriage contract a couple is simply living together. Would you loan money to someone without a contract? If you loan money without a contract, you might just as well call it a gift.

Contracts improve the chances that you will keep your end of the bargain because a contract spells out the expectations—in a way that can't be misunderstood—that both parties agree to. With a contract you can avoid miscommunication, confusion, or claims of "temporary insanity."

Bret and I prayed long and hard about the terms of our contract regarding my graduate-school education. I will share the answers we received because they applied perfectly when he was called to demanding Church service, and can be used by any couple where one member is called to a demanding Church position.

We felt the strong impression that I needed to do two things: (1) *schedule specific hours* to be away from the family rather than taking off arbitrarily when the need arose, and (2) when I was home, I needed to *schedule specific hours* to devote exclusively to my husband and children.

Since our children were in school for six hours a day, that gave me thirty hours a week with no regularly scheduled family responsibilities. I decided the family probably wouldn't suffer too much if I attended classes sometime during those thirty hours a week. Therefore, the specific hours I scheduled to be away from the family were the hours when my children were in school. And those were the *only* hours I would spend away. If I needed to attend a lab or a study group, I would do it during my specified "school" hours.

The second condition—scheduling specific hours to devote exclusively to the family—protected me from bringing work home and allowing it to infringe on our family life. Being home when the children were home was all well and good, but if I were to spend all my time studying, being home would not do a whole lot for my relationships with my husband and children. I knew that with the huge stack of books my professors required me to read and digest, my schoolwork would never be done. There would always be more to read. There would always be more to research. I would likely never feel I had completely mastered the material. If I waited until I was finished studying to spend time with the family, I knew I would never spend time with the family, because I would never finish studying. Therefore, I had to schedule time to devote exclusively to the family, even though my work was not done.

I decided to schedule Sundays exclusively as family time. During my undergraduate education, I had relied on Sundays to catch up on my studies. However, in my particular circumstance, I felt inspired to avoid studying on Sunday and to devote the day to my family.

CONTRACTS FOR CHURCH LEADERS

Because a contract proved so effective when I began my post-graduate studies in counseling, Bret and I decided to try something similar when he was called as a bishop. The specifics of the contract Bret and I devised are not nearly as important as the fact that we devised it together. We both signed it (literally—I have the original paper to this day), and we both felt good about it. The fact that we both agreed upon the contract is the secret to its success.

A contract between a husband and a wife who are steeped in Church service may look very much like my graduate school contract.

First, schedule *specific hours* for the Church leader to be away from home rather than jumping and running arbitrarily whenever a need arises. We recognized, however, that as bishop, Bret would need to be available for some emergencies.

Second, schedule *specific hours,* while at home, to devote exclusively to the family rather than spending every available minute on the telephone or working on the Church calling.

The same way graduate school could have consumed me, demanding callings can consume a Church member. If a Church leader allows a calling to take priority, and plans to devote every single second of the time left over from the calling to the family, that leader will discover there is not a single second left over for the family. Church leaders will always discover more people to fellowship, more people to visit, more people to teach. The job of a Church servant is never done.

When they begin a project, devoted Church servants may be tempted to give 150 percent. They can easily become galloping horses that leave their wagons broken down on the side of the road. Church leaders often have so much compassion and care about people so much that they could meet with struggling Saints until the wee hours of the morning, were they not bound by a contract to set limits.

Instead of giving the family the time left over after fulfilling a Church calling, devoted Church leaders can give a Church calling a specified amount of time even if everything isn't done. The family can then be the first priority, and time spent on a calling can be kept in check.

Sensitive after All

"A contract is so firm, so unyielding," you might lament.

Exactly. Contracts keep us honest. They prevent us from making excuses: "I didn't know it was that important to you," or "I thought you'd understand." Contracts keep us from *almost* making it home in time for the dinner party. Contracts help us keep our promises, not *almost* keep our promises.

Perhaps you have noticed that Heavenly Father is in favor of contracts. He calls them covenants. A covenant with deity is a contract you don't want to break. There is no room for "almost" in keeping covenants. There's room for repentance, of course, but the expectation is that each of us will keep our covenants fully. One of the reasons we trust Heavenly Father is that he has made the terms of his covenant perfectly clear and we know he will not break his promises.

The marriage covenant is an example of a contract with deity.

Baptismal covenants are contracts with deity. The covenants we make in the temple are contracts with deity. Notice that even in the case of these sacred covenants, certain elements of a contract prevail. There is more than one party to the covenant. Both parties pledge to keep that covenant. With the baptismal covenant, the pledge to keep the covenant comes when we walk into the water and become immersed. In the marriage covenant we utter words that indicate our intentions to keep the covenant. The temple recommend itself is a contract. When we sign our names at the bottom of the piece of paper that allows us to enter the sacred and holy temple, we are agreeing to keep the covenants we make in the temple.

WHY CONTRACTS WORK

The beauty of contracts is threefold.

1. A contract demands clear thinking from the individuals who sign the contract. In order to write something down on paper, you need to have a pretty clear idea about what's in your head. By writing your intentions down, you can make sure there is no confusion in your own mind as to what your responsibilities entail.

I was working with a father one time who complained that he couldn't discipline his son. When I asked him what he expected of the son, he said he expected the son to come home at a "reasonable time." When I asked him what the consequences were if the son wasn't home, he responded that the son would "get in trouble." It took me an entire session to get the father to pin down a "reasonable time" to 10:00 on weeknights and midnight on weekends. We had to schedule another appointment to decide what "get in trouble" meant to the dad. No wonder the son was confused. The dad was confused.

2. A contract prevents misunderstanding between parties. Both parties can see, in writing, what the other party is agreeing to do. Unless the language is deliberately vague and ambiguous, writing down your intentions on paper allows the other person to understand clearly what you plan to do. You can't say, "Oh, that's not what I meant," because you wrote it down in the first place and signed your name declaring what you meant. Miscommunication decreases with a contract. Both parties read the contract, and if one or the other doesn't understand what's written down, they rewrite it until they have a mutual understanding.

A verbal agreement is a contract too. It's not as formal as a written contract. It might seem that a verbal agreement should suffice and that a written agreement is unnecessary. That's true. A verbal agreement will suffice between a husband and a wife, and a handshake (or a kiss!) will seal the agreement, as long as there is absolutely no misunderstanding as to what is being agreed upon. But remember, communication between human beings is pretty tricky. Miscommunication occurs even when both parties maintain the purest of motives. A written contract simply protects two good people, both with honorable intentions, from misunderstanding one another.

3. Contracts spell out the consequences of keeping or not keeping an agreement. The contract specifies the reward each party will receive for keeping the contract and it states what will happen if either party fails to adhere to the terms of the contract. In the case of graduate school, if I kept my classes within the hours when the children were in school, Bret paid my tuition.

It's tempting to snivel at the prospect of rewards for good behavior. However, rewards are not a juvenile motivational technique saved for preschoolers. Each one of us works for rewards. We go to work because we receive a reward in the form of a paycheck. We keep the commandments because we want the reward of living with Heavenly Father again. Indeed, we may be motivated by higher principles than rewards. That's fabulous. In working out a schedule with a spouse, those who find they don't need rewards to motivate behavior may skip the rewards. But if either party finds it difficult to keep the terms of the contract, why not implement some rewards?

KEEPING THE CONTRACT

Whether individuals keep contracts because they want the rewards or because of personal integrity, the power of a contract will assure that the signatories go to great lengths to honor their part of the contract.

One time I missed an exam because of a family commitment. I knew it would be inconvenient to make up the exam, but I had committed to a family outing during the time the exam was administered, so I had to make arrangements to make up the exam.

The only time available to make up the exam was an afternoon when my kids were home from school and I was babysitting a neighbor, so I took all the children to the university with me. I planned to let them run on the campus green and throw a football while I sat on the grassy hill nearby and took the exam. The plan worked for about five questions. Campus security chased the children off the newly planted grass, and we all ended up in a tiny office on the third floor of the psych building.

There was nothing in the office except a table, a chair, a paper shredder, and a lot of shredded paper in bags. You can imagine how the children stayed entertained while I concentrated on my exam. Twenty-five questions were all it took for my children and the neighbor to cover the entire room with confetti they made out of the shredded paper. Confetti flew to the ceiling and covered the carpet. The children giggled as if they were playing in leaves on a crisp autumn day. I finished my exam, but they wanted to stay. So we stayed and, like the Cat in the Hat, vacuumed up all the evidence of our fun day. I'll never forget the price I paid to keep my family commitment.

Should an instance occur where you feel you can't keep the terms of the contract (such as if my professor would not let me make up a missed exam or if a Church leader was required to spend an unexpected evening away from the family), you can always renegotiate the contract or add an "emergency exceptions" clause. But both husband and wife will want to be part of the re-negotiation, so that neither experiences sorrow or disappointment at the unexpected intrusion into their plans.

AVOIDING DISAPPOINTMENT

The beauty of a contract, either written or unwritten, is that both parties know what to expect. Most of the disappointments we experience in life come not because we were let down but because we were let down when we never expected to be.

How would you feel if you made an offer on a house that cost $150,000 and when you went to closing, the owner asked you to pay $160,000? Even if you could afford the difference, you would be furious that you had budgeted for a certain payment that had now changed. What if you were supposed to move into the house on June first, and the day before you planned to move, the owner suddenly said you couldn't move in until June fifteenth? If you had known all along that you would not be able to move in until June fifteenth, you wouldn't be upset, but having to change plans—and especially having to change them at the last minute—would naturally raise your ire.

Couples in my practice become disappointed in one another most frequently not because something bad happened, but because something bad happened that they never expected to happen. They expected the best, and the worst occurred.

The wife who expects her husband to come home for dinner grows more and more agitated the longer he delays. However, if she knows not to expect him to return home until after a certain hour, she can plan her evening accordingly, and a nice evening it may turn out to be (almost anything is nicer than pacing the floor).

I used to throw a big birthday party for each of my children on his or her birthday. One year we invited the "alligator man" to display his collection of snakes, alligators, and various Florida reptiles at the birthday. Another year we rented the country club pool along with the lifeguards, who played games with the children. My children looked forward to their birthday parties enthusiastically all year long. Not only did they enjoy many creative and unusual themes, but they enjoyed the camaraderie of having all of their friends together at the same time.

Eventually, I grew utterly exhausted by the effort it took to dream up a theme for a new and unusual birthday party, to say nothing of the work it took to pull it off. So one year as the April birthdays drew near, my boys discovered they were not having a birthday party. Yes, there was weeping and wailing and gnashing of teeth. As we talked, I discovered the tears came not so much because they missed out on the birthday party, but because they had been so excited about it in the first place and their hopes had been dashed. Once they grew accustomed to the idea that their spectacular birthday parties were no more, they were content to enjoy a nice, quiet party with our immediate family. Getting their hopes dashed caused the greatest disappointment, not missing out on the party.

The contract between you and your spouse may or may not decrease the amount of time your spouse spends in Church service. Your spouse may still spend a great deal of time away, but the contract can make it easier to cope with those absences because the contract will

- inform you how much time your spouse will spend away
- tell you when your spouse will return
- determine how many people to plan for at meals and what to cook
- allow you to decide when to wait up and when to go to bed
- allow you to plan on alternative means of support (dinner companionship, someone to pick up milk, someone to help move furniture, or someone you can ask a particular question)

When your spouse's schedule is predictable, you may be disappointed because you can't enjoy his or her company, but you need not suffer the disappointment that occurs from botched plans. You do not experience unnecessary inconvenience (running to pick up a car pool in the middle of stirring a white sauce) or unexpected surprises (the science fair project your spouse dreamed up is due tomorrow, and you don't understand the theory of momentum in the least).

Contracts help you plan. They allow you to be in control of your own schedule instead of being at the mercy of an unpredictable and very demanding schedule.

Your contract with your spouse need not mirror the contract

we devised when Bret served as a bishop, but in case you're curious, the specifics of our contract were as follows:

1. Bret would spend all day Sunday at church, if necessary. He might leave before I awoke, and he might return after I went to sleep. I always knew not to count on a husband's company on Sunday. It was futile to try and stick my head in his office and wave, because there was usually a line outside the door. Occasionally, I would smile at him from my pew to let him know he was on my mind. It was a treat to see him grin back.

2. Bret decided to spend one evening a week at the church conducting interviews. He usually chose to conduct interviews the same night that the Scouts and the Young Women met so he could provide support to their activities when he had breaks between interviews. On the weeknights Bret spent at the church, we agreed he would leave to come home at 9:00 P.M.

3. Every third month, Bret conducted sacrament meeting. During the month he conducted, he was responsible for attending any events scheduled at the church and all of the youth activities scheduled anywhere else. This meant that he could be at youth conference one weekend, on a temple trip the next, basketball games the next. He attended every baptism during the month. (Our ward averaged twenty baptisms a year; that meant he attended an average of two baptisms during the month he conducted.) He also attended Relief Society enrichment meeting, which was always on a separate night from the youth activities; this meant he was gone at least two weekday evenings. He also cooked breakfast for the seminary students once during the month. His counselors made the same commitment every third month when it was their turn to conduct.

We always sat down during family home evening on Monday night to review our schedules for the week. This was essential, particularly during a conducting month, so I would not suffer any surprises. Even during a conducting month, Bret agreed to leave his meetings by 9:00, so as not to keep me up late. (I kept inviting him to call another early-morning seminary teacher, so I wouldn't have to go to bed so early. He declined.) You could also include elements in your contract that govern non-church related activities too, such as days to work late or play golf. But we had long-ago negotiated those details, so they weren't part of the contract necessitated by a demanding Church calling.

Surprises will still occur even with a contract between husband and wife. People get sick and need blessings. However, it will be easier for a spouse to cope when the Church servant is called out on an emergency because true emergencies don't happen that often. A wife's ability to trust her husband and a husband's ability to trust his wife will grow because, barring a rare emergency, the Church leader keeps the terms of the contract.

THE OTHER SIDE OF THE STORY

As with any contract, responsibility extends to both parties. The obvious responsibility of the Church leader is to keep the schedule proposed in the contract. He or she will leave the family to perform Church duties only during the hours specified in the contract. In exchange, the spouse makes certain promises. The most important of all promises a spouse can make to a busy Church servant is to agree to support him or her.

You discovered at the beginning of this book that support comes in many shapes and sizes. You may choose to support at one of the deeper levels discussed previously, such as listening well, bearing one another's burdens, encouraging your spouse, caring about the same sheep. Even if a marital companion doesn't choose to provide this extensive amount of support, at the very least he or she can avoid placing roadblocks in the path of the Church leader.

It is also essential that you not tear your spouse down. This means if the Church leader you support keeps his or her part of the contract, you must agree not to complain about the hours he or she spends serving the Lord, particularly when you signed a contract agreeing to those hours in the first place. Whatever else you do to truly support a valiant Church leader, it is essential that you not grumble about the terms of the contract you helped draft.

Nothing slows a Church leader down as effectively as someone clinging to his or her heels as he or she attempts to gallop forward. It's hard enough to leave the happy family swimming together in the pool in order to go home teaching. It's nearly impossible for a Church leader to leave the happy family swimming together in the pool when the family is begging the leader to stay or pouting as he goes.

Church servants also find it difficult to leave when they know they will return to negative salutations. Negative salutations may pop out of our mouths without warning: "So, you finally decided to come home." "It's about time you graced our threshold with your shadow." "Well, I didn't know you still lived here." Such greetings, whether blatantly negative or slyly sarcastic, weigh a Church servant down, just like the verbal "clinging to the leg" he received as he walked out the door.

THE REWARD

Loving feelings between a husband and wife involved in Church service increase a hundredfold when both of them keep the simplest contract. When a Church leader keeps a predictable schedule, and his or her spouse resists complaining about that schedule, they will avoid loads of negative feelings. Harmony in a couple's marriage may be reward enough for them both to keep the terms of the contract. Then, whatever rewards are drafted into the contract will merely be icing on top of an already harmonious relationship.

CHAPTER 9

FAITH IN YOUR SPOUSE'S GOOD JUDGMENT

ONE FRIDAY EVENING MY HUSBAND AND I WERE enjoying a quiet dinner, away from home, with our cellular phones turned off. We had chosen a restaurant at a very secluded resort hotel because the chances of bumping into someone we knew at this restaurant were slim. I had been waiting all week for some private time with my husband to discuss some very real concerns. Before our main course was even served, the waiter asked my husband to come to the phone.

Bret returned to the table and announced that he had to leave. Someone in our ward had been taken to the hospital. We paid for our appetizer and quietly walked to the car. He opened my door so I could get in, and we drove home in silence. I didn't want to say anything because I couldn't think of anything nice to say. I was wrapped up in my own sorrow. I was feeling deprived because it seemed I could never have a moment alone with my own husband. I felt cheated and more than a tad resentful. People were going to the hospital all the time in our ward. Why did this have to happen in the middle of our date, the only time I saw my husband alone all week? Why couldn't someone else in the ward go to the hospital to offer comfort?

I tucked myself in bed, failing to say my prayers because I still couldn't think of anything nice to say. I tossed and turned, tore the sheets from the mattress, and soaked a few pillows with tears. About three o'clock in the morning my husband called. One of the young men in our ward who was a very talented gymnast had been practicing during a Friday "free" night at the gym. A triple back flip in the air ended in disaster. This vibrant young man slammed his head on the mat and broke his neck. My husband had waited at the hospital all night while surgeons operated, set the bones in the boy's neck, and placed a halo brace around his skull so he couldn't move his head. Our gymnastics star was paralyzed from the neck down.

I dropped to my knees and this time I prayed. The prayer was far different from the one I had pondered but skipped five hours earlier. Instead of expressing resentment because I had to share my husband so frequently with so many, I expressed gratitude for a righteous husband who could provide comfort in such a terrible time of need.

Perhaps my attitude would have changed without my knowing where my husband had been all night. Eventually I would have licked my wounds and stopped feeling sorry for myself. However, a little knowledge changed my feelings instantly.

Every time you send your husband or wife out the door (or out of the restaurant!) to render service, you give a gift to the Lord. You perform your own small act of service by sharing your beloved with the members of your congregation. You share your spouse with mothers, fathers, children, grandparents, and so many others who are in need of the counsel only an ecclesiastical leader ordained of God can give.

Giving up my husband in the middle of our date became far easier when I learned where my gift had gone. I am grateful that my spouse cared enough to phone me in the middle of this sad situation and let me know why he had walked out in the middle of our date.

It is not always possible, however, for an ecclesiastical leader to share with a supportive spouse the nature of his service. You may send your husband out the door and never know how he spends his time.

Much of the service your spouse renders will be confidential in nature, and you will not know where your gift is going. At times this may be troubling; the spouse who once shared everything with you is now bound to carry alone some of the burdens, information, and sorrows of his calling.

Elder Jeffrey R. Holland told a similar story that began, again, with a simple phone call:

> May I share just one contemporary example of both the challenge and blessings that our "calls to serve" can bring. A wonderful sister recently said to a dear friend: "I want to tell you about the moment I ceased resenting my husband's time and sacrifice as a bishop. It had seemed uncanny how an 'emergency' would arise with a ward member just when he and I were about to go out to do something special together.
>
> "One day I poured out my frustration, and my husband agreed we should guarantee, in addition to Monday nights, one additional night a week just for us. Well, the first 'date night' came, and we were about to get into the car for an evening together when the telephone rang.

"'This is a test,' I smiled at him. The telephone kept ringing. 'Remember our agreement. Remember our date. Remember me. Let the phone ring.' In the end I wasn't smiling.

"My poor husband looked trapped between me and a ringing telephone. I really did know that his highest loyalty was to me, and I knew he wanted that evening as much as I did. But he seemed paralyzed by the sound of that telephone.

" 'I'd better at least check,' he said with sad eyes. 'It is probably nothing at all.'

" 'If you do, our date is ruined,' I cried. 'I just know it.'

"He squeezed my hand and said, 'Be right back,' and he dashed in to pick up the telephone.

"Well, when my husband didn't return to the car immediately, I knew what was happening. I got out of the car, went into the house, and went to bed. The next morning he spoke a quiet apology, I spoke an even quieter acceptance, and that was the end of it.

"Or so I thought. I found the event still bothering me several weeks later. I wasn't blaming my husband, but I was disappointed nevertheless. The memory was still fresh when I came upon a woman in the ward I scarcely knew. Very hesitantly, she asked for the opportunity to talk. She then told of becoming infatuated with another man, who seemed to bring excitement into her life of drudgery, she with a husband who worked full-time and carried a full load of classes at the university. Their apartment was confining. She had small children who were often demanding, noisy, and exhausting. She said: 'I was sorely tempted to leave what I saw as my wretched state and just go with this man. My situation was such that I felt I deserved better than what I had. My rationalization persuaded me to think I could walk away from my husband, my children, my temple covenants, and my Church and find happiness with a stranger.'

"She said: 'The plan was set; the time for my escape was agreed upon. Yet, as if in a last gasp of sanity, my conscience told me to call your husband, my bishop. I say "conscience," but I know that was a spiritual prompting directly from heaven. Almost against my will, I called. The telephone rang and rang and rang. Such was the state of my mind that I actually thought, "If the bishop doesn't answer, that will be a sign I should go through with my plan." The phone kept ringing, and I was about to hang up and walk straight into destruction when suddenly I heard your husband's voice. It penetrated my soul like lightning. Suddenly I heard myself sobbing, saying, "Bishop, is that you? I am in trouble. I need help." Your husband came with help, and I am safe today because he answered that telephone.

" 'I look back and realize I was tired and foolish and vulnerable. I love my husband and my children with all my heart. I can't imagine the tragedy my life would be without them. These are still demanding times for our family. I know everyone has them. But we have addressed some of these issues, and things are looking brighter. They always do eventually.' Then she said: 'I don't know you well, but I wish to thank you for supporting your husband in his calling. I don't know what the cost for such service has been to you or to your children, but if on a difficult day there is a particularly personal cost, please know how eternally grateful I will be for the sacrifice people like you make to help rescue people like me'" (*Trusting Jesus* [Salt Lake City: Deseret Book, 2003], 111–13).

Elder Holland continued by saying, "Because I am adamant about spouses and children deserving sacred, committed time with a husband and father, nine times out of ten I would have been right alongside that wife telling her husband not to answer that telephone. But I am as grateful in my own way as that young woman was in hers that in this instance this good man followed the prompting of the Spirit and responded to his 'call'—in this case, literally—his 'call to serve'" (*Trusting Jesus,* 113).

There will be times that you watch your Church-servant spouse walk out the door without any knowledge of where he is going or what he is doing. The service your spouse is rendering may be of a confidential nature, and unless the person being served reveals the nature of the service to you, as did the woman in Elder Holland's story, you will never know of it.

For some, this can be one of the most difficult challenges of supporting a spouse in his or her Church service. Not knowing where your spouse has gone to serve requires a great deal of faith in the Lord's servant. When it is not possible for the Church leader to disclose the nature of the service rendered, because of confidentiality requirements, it requires that you exercise faith that your spouse is not leaving you and the children for a trivial reason.

When your spouse spends an inordinate amount of time serving, have faith that it is for something absolutely crucial. Should your spouse leave you abruptly at an inopportune time, or miss a highly significant event, know that only a true emergency would draw him or her away.

If you have faith in your spouse's good judgment, and your relationship is built on understanding and trust, and both of you rely on the promptings of the Spirit, you will feel comfort when your spouse is away on the Lord's errand—even if you do not know the specific nature of that errand.

TAKING ADVANTAGE OF YOUR GIFT

Sadly, in some marriages there may be reason for a spouse to lack faith that her gift of sharing her partner is going to a worthwhile cause. Though difficult to imagine, some husbands and wives deliberately use Church service as an excuse to stay away from home. Church service is a clever way for people to spend their time if they don't enjoy being at home but don't want to appear selfish. How can you argue with a Church servant who goes about doing good in the world? It's not like the servant is out all night playing poker or sitting at a sports bar; after all, the servant is out serving his or her fellowman. Were you to open your mouth to complain, you would feel like the villain, a Lex Luthor, thwarting the plans of a major do-gooder. However, a Church servant who uses Church service as an excuse to stay away from home because he or she can't deal with family life may not be a superhero after all.

In an *Ensign* article some years ago, a Church leader in Los Angeles observed: "I have seen men who were incapable of dealing with their family responsibilities and who used church work as an excuse. I am as impatient with that as I am with the man who uses his business as a pretext for not taking care of his family and his church responsibilities" (Howard B. Anderson, quoted in

Herbert F. Murray, "A Time for Every Needful Thing," *Ensign*, September 1971, 15).

If you suspect that your spouse is using Church service as an excuse not to spend time at home, you must question his or her absence. You would be exercising blind faith to watch your spouse go out the door, knowing it will be to the detriment of your relationship.

Suspicion that your spouse does not spend his or her time responsibly may be justified for another reason besides the servant's apparent desire to avoid home and family. Perhaps your spouse wants to stay home. You have a wonderful relationship. You would rather spend time together than with anyone else on the planet, yet still you suspect him or her of staying away longer than wise or necessary. You suspect that your spouse may spend excessive hours away from home, not because he or she wants to be away, but because the members monopolize his or her time.

Members may ask a bishop or an elders quorum president to help in ways that are beyond the scope of the leader's calling. Members may attempt to take advantage of the Church leader's generosity. They may ask for thirty minutes, then swallow up hours of his time. Individuals who have not had access to emotional resources throughout their lives may feel like a kid in a candy shop when they meet a Latter-day Saint. All of a sudden they encounter kind, caring people who pay attention to them. They soak it up like sunshine in Paris. They want to wallow in it, relish it, and never let it go. Sometimes they make an appointment to see the bishop, not because they want help with repentance or some legitimate need, but because they crave attention and positive affirmation.

A supportive spouse may have faith in a Church leader's desire to budget time appropriately but lack faith in the members' willingness to respect a leader's time. The spouse may suspect Church members of being oblivious to their leader's needs or those of the family. A spouse may notice when a highly compassionate Church leader is being taken advantage of. If this is the case, he or she could very gently suggest this possibility to the Church leader and allow the Church leader to assess the validity of the observation and respond appropriately.

For the most part, once you and your Church-servant spouse have reserved specific times of the week for family activities and others for Church service, you'll naturally fall into a rhythm that supports your spouse's calling and your family's need for time together. Most couples will also come to an understanding that emergencies happen, and they happen at inopportune times. That is the nature of an emergency. If it could wait for a better time, it wouldn't be an emergency.

Rather than feeling sorry for themselves or angry with their beloved Church servant for missing an important engagement, most spouses will learn to deal well with emergencies, especially if the Church servant checks in occasionally or can provide estimates of when he or she will arrive home.

YOU DON'T WANT TO KNOW

As difficult as it is to send your loved one off not knowing whom he is going to serve, it may be even more difficult knowing the nature of the service. Even though the Church servant you support will not be able to share confidential information with you, the members themselves may choose to share information with you. In addition, you may stumble across information inadvertently. People will leave messages for you to pass along to your spouse and will reveal details you didn't bargain for. They may call seeking your spouse and, finding him or her unavailable, provide you with a description of their plight. You may inadvertently overhear a conversation, view a name on the caller ID, or answer the door when someone stops by for an interview or to pick up an item. You may arrive home and find someone sitting in your driveway, waiting for your spouse. Whether you try to or not, you will likely learn some things that need to remain confidential.

My dear friend has served twice as a bishop's wife, in two different wards. She begs her husband to call her to serve in the nursery. "That way I'm completely out of the loop. I won't know what's happening unless it's printed on a flyer."

The difficulty with stumbling across confidential information is holding it. You are unprepared to receive it. You don't know what to do with it. It's not your responsibility to hold. It can be overwhelming to possess. Your tendency is to get rid of it so it doesn't burden you.

You may feel as I did once when I was a teenager working in the file room of the radiology department at LDS Hospital in Salt Lake City. I arrived at work one morning and on my way to the file room I passed a woman sitting in a wheelchair waiting for an X ray. She wore an open hospital gown, and her head was completely bald. She was very old, and very sick. She had been coughing up blood and mucus into a tissue as I walked by. Suddenly she stopped me. "Can you take this for me?" she asked and handed me the tissue soaked with illness. I was totally unprepared for her to give me this responsibility. I was just a file clerk and not supposed to be involved in direct patient care. I didn't know what to do with this responsibility and I couldn't wait to get rid of it.

I learned two principles on this occasion that seem highly applicable to information that might be thrust upon us against our will. First, we shouldn't form judgments about the person who is sick. We are not the doctor. We are just the person walking down the hall. Second, it's not an act of kindness to pass the sick tissue on to anyone else.

The Responsibility Not to Judge

"You will learn things about people you wish you never knew," a sage priesthood leader told my husband when he was called to serve as bishop. "You will also learn things about people you wish everybody knew."

You, too, may learn things about people you wish you never knew. You may learn things by accident, or people may choose to tell you their stories. It will hurt to imagine some of the anguish these people have suffered, both as a result of their own mistakes and as a result of circumstances out of their control. Your heart may ache as you hear their stories and you may wish you had never learned what you know. Yet the resiliency of the human spirit and the bravery these individuals exhibit in overcoming their challenges will thrill your soul, and you will wish you could tell everybody about their triumphs.

You must be very careful, however, that if you learn a little bit about someone you don't jump to conclusions or make judgments about them. People are complex, and life has so many twists and turns; it's hard to ever see a situation accurately.

A man who once came into my office for counseling had black, rotting teeth right in the front of his mouth. My first thought was, "Why doesn't he get those teeth fixed? He has a good job with benefits; he could put a little money away each month and pay for some dental work. This is really disgusting to look at." A few sessions later the man revealed, without my asking, that he hated his teeth. He had considered dental work; however, his wife's parents lived in the Philippines, and every month he sent them money, without which they would not survive.

Shouldering that responsibility, he could not afford to spend money on his teeth. Needless to say, my impression of him changed considerably. I simply had not known enough about this man to form an accurate impression.

The spouses of Church leaders may stumble across some information, but seldom have access to the quantity of information afforded a professional counselor or an ecclesiastical leader. Still, you may be tempted to form judgments about others based on limited information and an even more limited capacity to judge.

Your trustworthiness as the spouse of a Church leader includes not only your ability to refrain from spreading confidential information but also your ability to refrain from thinking judgmentally about the people your spouse serves. We mortals are in no position to assess why people get themselves into the circumstances they are in, or whose fault it is that they are in those circumstances. Your judgments may be critical or sympathetic. It doesn't matter. You must refrain from making value judgments at all.

One Authorized Judge

When you stumble across a little information, you have an enormous responsibility to avoid making a judgment based on that information. No matter how much information you possess as the spouse of a Church leader, you are never in a position to make a judgment as to a person's worthiness or unworthiness. Elder Dallin H. Oaks teaches us that, while we are required to make "intermediate judgments" about others, none of us is in a position to make final judgments (see " 'Judge Not' and Judging," *Ensign*, August 1999, 7–13).

No one has the authority to judge a person's standing in the Church. You will not be blessed with inspiration or insight to make that kind of judgment because it is not your calling. Neither will you want to judge a person's moral character, because you do not have the capacity to decide if someone is good or bad, worthy or unworthy, capable of salvation or not.

In fact, the only one who can truly judge an individual's moral character, whether a person is good or bad, worthy of salvation or not, is the Savior of mankind. Only Jesus Christ truly knows our hearts, has taken our pains upon himself, has experienced every emotion we have experienced, has endured our every trial, and knows our chemical makeup. He is the great physician who understands thoroughly our illness and knows the cure.

Playing It "Safe"

Stumbling upon information that you didn't bargain for can be overwhelming, and you might want to get rid of it as quickly as possible. However, it is your responsibility, when you are married to a Church leader, to dispose of the information appropriately. Obviously, you will not share information with anybody other than your spouse, who has the stewardship and the skills to deal with the information.

To make sure I don't accidentally reveal information that belongs in a confidential setting, I have chosen not to reveal any information regarding my husband's Church calling. Even when I discover innocuous information—like "guess who's getting married," or "guess who's having a baby"—I want to reassure members that I am not an information spreader by avoiding all discussions about topics related to my spouse's calling. A poignant experience from my past helped me believe that we can never be too careful when it comes to keeping confidences.

Once when I was in high school I was presented with some information I thought was common knowledge. The parents of one of my good friends were getting divorced and someone stopped me in the hall at school to reveal the information. Utterly naïve to the fact that this information might be gossip, I approached my good friend later that day and expressed my condolences.

"I'm so sorry to hear about your parents," I told Carol.

"What about my parents?" she asked.

"I understand they are getting divorced."

"They are not!" she exclaimed. "Who told you that?" She stormed away in tears.

In fact, Carol's parents truly were getting divorced, but she had not been told. I felt terrible. I had broken this devastating news, news that was not mine to break. I felt like an orderly telling a family their loved one had passed away when the surgeon should have broken the news.

Later that day, the girl who told me about the divorce approached me angrily. "Why did you tell Carol about her parents?" she asked me. "Didn't you know that was a secret?"

I couldn't imagine how the general public could possibly know such important information before the children themselves. But such was the case.

This devastating experience taught me to be extremely careful about the information I chose to share. Even information you think is not confidential might be. That is why I reiterate, the safest policy is to refuse to be the bearer of information it is not your responsibility to bear, particularly when people may blurt out confidences to you, as the spouse of a Church leader.

Although you may be the recipient of some information, you will be the purveyor of none. You are like a safe-deposit box: no one can access your information except the person who put it in the box. You are not an ATM, where all kinds of people come to make withdrawals. The only one who can access you, the safe-deposit box, is the depositor.

Lonely at the Top

Individuals who enjoy intimacy in relationships know that sharing information promotes that intimacy. In order to make friends, or to grow closer to someone, people share information of a private nature. The more intimate the information shared, the closer the individuals feel.

I know several Relief Society sisters who "walk and talk" every morning. They stay in shape, and they stay entertained with conversation during the walk. These sisters have in common their membership in the Church and their association with all the same people. Conversing about ward members and their lives and their callings seems natural to them.

Outsiders who talk about people can do little harm. Like owners of stock in the same company, you may discuss how the company is being run or the direction the market is heading, and all your talk is merely speculation. However, if one of you is married to an officer in the company—exposed to the particulars about how the company is being run, of pending mergers or acquisitions, of profits or losses—and you discuss these with your walking partner, you could be guilty of insider trading and subject to criminal charges.

Likewise, with a husband or wife who is a leader in the Church, you may be exposed to insider information. Your peers will realize that you possess more information than heretofore. They should respect your position and should not expect you to converse freely about your spouse's calling. It may feel lonely at the top, but you will be respected for keeping quiet and remaining uncritical.

CHAPTER 10

LIGHTEN YOUR OWN LOAD

IN OUR SOCIETY WE ARE GENERALLY QUITE compassionate with one another when we experience individual stressors. Our colleagues readily give us permission to function at less than full capacity during a trying time.

The birth of a baby, for example, is a delightful event—and one that produces a measure of stress. At such times we accept that other tasks be put aside while we celebrate and adjust to the new spirit that has entered our lives.

Marriages—pleasant as they may be—and the accompanying celebration can also cause their measure of stress. Planning a wedding may require that the bride or groom, or the parents of the bride and groom, put other priorities on hold for a time while they concentrate on celebrating this highly significant union.

Moving to a new location to accept a career promotion is also stressful and forces the relocated family to concentrate on getting settled, putting other priorities aside for a period of time.

In addition to receiving compassion from our colleagues

when we experience pleasant life stressors, we generally experience compassion from our colleagues when trauma enters our lives. I'll never forget the day I turned on the news and saw a passenger jet disappear into one of the twin towers of the World Trade Center. Flames exploded from the side of the building; I felt as if I had been punched in the stomach, and I became too weak to stand.

Much of America felt as I did that day. Many left work and went home. Parents took their children out of school. Employees who stayed in the workplace gathered at the water cooler and talked. Little work was done. Our bosses and our friends allowed us to cease functioning for a while and deal with this crisis.

No one expects us to perform to our usual standards when we are experiencing a crisis. When a loved one dies we give up many of our normal responsibilities to mourn the death. We are excused from our usual routine when we have experienced a major trauma. Our friends say: "Go home early," "Take a few days off," or "Sit down and talk with me for a while."

Supporting a spouse who is serving in the kingdom, and serving alongside our spouses, can provide stress in our lives. It may be pleasant stress, such as with the birth of a baby or the wedding of a child, or it may be traumatic, such as the death of a loved one or a bout with a long illness. Not only does the type of stress we experience vary, but the intensity of the stress also varies. Your stress may be significant, or it may be minor.

Whatever the intensity of your stress, you will probably find it necessary to take steps to adjust your lifestyle in order to deal with the stress. President Ezra Taft Benson's sage counsel to "pray as though everything depend[s] upon God and work as though everything depends on you" can apply readily to Church leaders and their supportive companions (*So Shall Ye Reap,* comp. Reed A. Benson [Salt Lake City: Deseret Book, 1960], 165). There are many steps you can take to alleviate your stress. Then when you have done your part, you can be assured the Lord will come to your aid.

JUST IN TIME

I testify that Heavenly Father will come to the rescue when you have done everything you can to make service in the kingdom possible. However, if you fail to do your part, to work with your whole heart and mind, it's a little audacious to pray for Heavenly Father to come to your rescue. When you have trimmed and cropped your own schedules appropriately, and you still struggle with your calling, you can approach Heavenly Father with full confidence that he will make it possible to fulfill your responsibility in building the kingdom here on this earth.

At the time my eldest son entered seminary, I was called to serve as an early-morning seminary teacher. I really struggled with the calling. Rising so early was not easy for me, and finding time each day to prepare a quality lesson along with all my other responsibilities thoroughly overwhelmed me.

One morning I rose to the sound of the alarm, and on the way to the bathroom I was so tired I ran into the corner of a wall. Yes, it was pretty funny—running into a wall. However, I met the wall right at the eyebrow and it split open my forehead and blood began streaming down my face. Even with an ice pack, I could not stop the bleeding unless I lay down flat. My husband awoke and called all the students to cancel seminary that morning.

Thoroughly exhausted, and overwhelmed to the point of tears, I fell upon my knees and pled with my Heavenly Father for strength beyond my own. There was no way a human being could possibly keep the schedule I was keeping on the amount of sleep I was getting. I needed a miracle, and I was asking for one.

Our dear Father heard my plea and answered my prayer. I felt impressed that there were some activities consuming my life that I needed to forgo for the present time. I needed to concentrate on the task in front of me first and foremost. Once I had done everything I could do, he would carry me the rest of the way.

I immediately eliminated as many of the responsibilities as I could that were consuming my time, but I was still pretty overloaded. My husband was still the bishop, I still had four children, and although I was able to reduce my caseload, I worked part-time as a counselor.

After I had done everything I felt the Lord wanted me to do in order to fulfill my seminary calling, He did the rest. I began to wake at 5:00 A.M. completely refreshed. The sleep I was able to receive restored my energy like it never had before. My lessons came together with less preparation. In the four years I taught, I never again had to cancel a class and I never missed a day of seminary because of illness. A small scar in the center of my right eyebrow reminds me to this day where to turn when I hit the wall.

Perhaps many of you have experienced miracles such as this. Elder Henry B. Eyring, as quoted by Jeannene N. Barton in her talk "The Balanced Woman," given at the 2000 CES New Testament Conference, calls this Heavenly Father's "just in time" policy. When you have done everything you can do, and you reach the end of your rope, and your arms are weak and you think you are destined to fall into the abyss below, here comes the aid and assistance of your Heavenly Father, carrying you to safety.

The sacrifice you have been asked to make perhaps seems greater than your ability, and indeed, it may be. However, it is not greater than the ability of our Heavenly Father.

Regardless of the depth or breadth of the sacrifice your own family makes to support a valiant Church servant, Heavenly

Father will provide you with the means to render the service to which your family has been called. Those who ask for help with faith in Heavenly Father's desire to come to their aid will assuredly receive a miraculous rescue, "just in time."

DRAWING THE LINE

Consider the following diagrams as a model of an individual's capacity to serve. Let's say that one end of a scale represents the attention we must pay to our own needs, such as physical fitness, personal scripture study, home maintenance, and all else we have the opportunity to do to meet our own needs. The other end of the scale represents the attention we choose to pay to other people's needs, such as volunteering our services as a baby-sitter or a maintenance man.

The line we draw between attending to our own needs and attending to the needs of others fluctuates, depending on how smoothly things are running in our own lives. When things are going great in your own life, you can move the line far to the left, attending little to your own needs and a lot to the needs of others. When your own life is filled with stress, either pleasant or unpleasant, you will find it necessary to move the line farther to the right, as you expend more energy attending to your own needs and less energy attending to the needs of others.

The line you draw between the attention an individual gives to his or her own needs and the attention that person gives to the needs of others will move constantly. You will need to consider

YOUR LIFE IS CHALLENGING AT THE MOMENT

Effort Spent Meeting Your Own Needs	*Others' Needs*

YOUR LIFE IS RUNNING RELATIVELY SMOOTHLY

Your Own Needs	*Effort Spent Meeting Others' Needs*

how smoothly things are going in your own life in order to determine how much service you can afford to render to others.

During those times when your life is relatively free of stress, you will be in a position to focus on others. You might invite the new family in the ward over for dinner, or organize a neighborhood ball game for family home evening, or throw a baby shower for a new mother and hand-crochet an afghan for a gift. However, when you are experiencing a great deal of stress in your own life, you probably won't invite company for dinner. If you're like me, you'll probably be driving through McDonald's to buy Happy Meals. Instead of organizing a neighborhood ball game, you might crash on the sofa and watch a ball game on television. Instead of throwing a baby shower and hand-crocheting an afghan for the baby, you might buy a gift and send it to the shower with someone else who is attending. During stressful times it is best for you to focus primarily on the necessary responsibilities, rather than the optional.

Granted, these are extreme examples of both self-focus and other-focus. Most of the time the line you draw won't be at either extreme on the continuum. Usually the stressful times in life aren't hugely stressful. Minor stress is far more common. When encountering lesser stressors, you might move the line only a notch or two. The line might hover around the center of the continuum. When you encounter a difficult situation you might move the line just a notch or two to the right so you can expend more energy meeting your own needs and a little less meeting others' needs.

During a time of minor stress you might not need to take three or four days off work, but you may find it necessary to buy lasagna for the new mother rather than cooking a homemade lasagna.

Elder M. Russell Ballard counsels, "Recognize limitations; no one can do everything. When you have done the best you can, be satisfied and don't look back and second-guess, wondering how you could have done more. Be at peace within yourselves" ("Be an Example of the Believers," *Ensign*, November 1991, 95).

It's perfectly acceptable to make adjustments in your level of service according to the level of stress you face in life. Don't wait for a major personal trauma as an excuse to slow down and focus on your own needs. If you adjust your output, taking into consideration both minor and moderate stressors in your own life, you can avoid needlessly inviting a major stressor.

LIGHTEN YOUR OWN LOAD

The most obvious consequence of living with a spouse who doesn't spend a great deal of time at home is that he or she may not be able to contribute to the functioning of the household as in the days B.C. (before calling). Some of the family responsibilities he or she used to assume may now fall on your shoulders. If your spouse used to get up in the morning, pack lunches, dress the children, and walk them to the bus stop, but can no longer do that, you now have a lot more to do from 6:00 A.M. to 8:00 A.M. If your spouse used to drive car pools or help with homework, but can't help in this manner anymore, you now have a lot more work to do from 6:00 P.M. to 8:00 P.M. A spouse who is called to serve the Lord in a demanding capacity simply leaves you with a longer "to do" list.

Since you are carrying a portion of your spouse's load, your own load may become too heavy to bear. Naturally this requires a lightening of your own load. During this particular period of life, while you are supporting a spouse in his or her Church service, your own agenda will change. Time doesn't exist to do all the things you used to do or all the things you want to do. You will need to attend to the necessary tasks and leave the optional ones for another season.

Should your loved one be off serving the Lord, you may have to drive the car pools, but you don't necessarily have to cook elaborate meals. You may have to help all the kids with their homework, but you can usually justify missing the PTA meeting. Because you spent time reading the bedtime stories and tucking the children into bed, you may let yourself off the hook when you don't take the time to write all the missionaries serving from your ward. You can't do everything. Each of us is just one person. And those supporting a spouse with a demanding Church calling have a highly legitimate a reason for not doing everything.

A TIME AND SEASON FOR ALL THINGS

"Every week the calendars circulate in Relief Society. Sisters sign up to feed the missionaries, they sign up to bring casseroles to new mothers, they sign up to work at the cannery, or they sign up to sew quilts at the stake center," said the wife of one busy Church servant. "Every week I pass the calendars along with a twinge of remorse.

"Inviting missionaries over for the holidays used to delight our family. Our three boys saw close-up what missionaries do on their missions. Our sons became close to the elders, who frequently wrote to our sons after they returned home. The missionaries always brought little games to our home. I felt like Betty Crocker when they visited because no one else appreciated my cooking the way the elders did. They left spiritual messages and we were uplifted by their visits.

"We tried and tried to invite the missionaries over once my husband received his calling, and I found myself canceling over and over. He was usually detained at the church. Sometimes we could not find a single night of the week when our family would all be home to eat together. Having the missionaries over for dinner was an optional task that we had to give up for a season."

One sister gave up working in the classroom during her husband's tenure as elders quorum president. She found she was spending so much time taking the grandmothers to the doctor and taking broken items in for repair—things her husband used to do—that she needed to lighten her own schedule. She started applying the guideline suggested for busy servants of the Lord: "Do what only you can do."

Another sister gave up sewing. She used to make the drapes and bedspreads that decorated her home. She saved a lot of money this way, and she showed her devotion to her family. However, she put this activity on hold while her husband was heavily involved in service to the Lord. There would always be bare windows to dress.

WHAT GIVES?

Just exactly how do you slow down and attend to the demands of having a frequently unavailable spouse? Which activities should you give up so you don't become overwhelmed?

Each of us will identify different responsibilities that make us feel overwhelmed and therefore will lighten our loads in different ways. One individual might choose to eliminate an early morning run because it is just one more thing to fit into his schedule. Another individual may thrive on a morning run to gear up for the day's added responsibilities. One individual might choose to stop cooking elaborate meals because cooking is burdensome, while another individual may find cooking an indulgence that helps her feel better in the absence of a spouse.

Pay close attention to your feelings as you go about your tasks. Determine which tasks help you feel more energetic and which tasks wear you out. Those tasks that weigh you down may be the ones you want to eliminate, if at all possible, when you are under stress. The activities that boost your spirits and augment your energy will be the activities you want to keep—and perhaps indulge in even more often.

CHAPTER 11

SERVE WITHIN
YOUR MEANS

IN CHAPTER THREE WE LEARNED THAT HUSBANDS
and wives who are equally yoked serve in the kingdom with the
same enthusiasm, the same level of devotion. A husband may
home teach a new family and his wife will invite them over for
family home evening. A wife may visit teach a sister, and her husband will mow the sister's lawn. A wife may organize a girls' camp
and the husband chaperone. A husband may baptize a new convert and the wife give a talk at the baptism. We know service is
sweeter when shared with a friend. Working side by side in this
great cause strengthens that friendship with your spouse.

Supporting a spouse means both husband and wife serve the
Lord. So if your husband is anxiously engaged in the work, you
will elect to be anxiously engaged too. With two anxiously
engaged servants in your home, you may be a tad anxious at the
depth and breadth of the responsibility that prevails in both of
your lives. Your own plate will fill up rapidly, and you will be
challenged to find moderation.

My husband and I have tried hard to discover balance while both immersed in service to the Lord. Living in Florida magnified this challenge.

We both grew up in the desert, so when we moved to Florida we were completely enchanted with all the water that surrounded us. We bought a house two miles from the Atlantic Ocean and a half-mile from the Intracoastal Waterway. We lived on a navigable river, deep enough to pull skiers and narrow enough that the wind seldom churned up waves. Within an hour's drive, freshwater lakes, with cabins along the shores and white sandy beaches, were abundant. We absolutely could not resist buying a boat.

Our stake president laughed when he learned we had purchased a boat. "Mormons do not know how to use a boat properly," he warned us. He was right. Our little bow rider spent most of its life in our garage while Bret spent his weekends on Scout campouts or moving furniture with the elders quorum. Any boater knows that to use a boat "properly" you launch it Friday after work and don't pull it out of the water until the weekend is over, late Sunday night. Believing, behaving, and serving Latter-day Saints certainly do not use a boat the way the rest of the world uses a boat.

Does this mean Latter-day Saints have no business owning boats? I hope not. We all need some "R and R" in order to keep our batteries charged. However, we don't spend the entire weekend on the water the way many avid boaters do. Finding a way to serve with all your heart, might, mind, and strength and still take time to recharge your batteries can prove to be quite a balancing act. You must relax a bit in order to have the energy to serve; yet, any time you spend attending to your own needs is time you could spend attending to someone else's needs. How can you balance your capacity for giving when faced with the host of needs out there? I believe the answer is found by studying the principle of self-reliance.

SERVE WITHIN YOUR MEANS

For years the Brethren have counseled the Latter-day Saints to live within their means. They counsel us to get out of debt and to get an education so we can support our families; they counsel us not to go into debt except for a home and an education. The poorest Saint and the richest Saint receive the same counsel—live within your means and don't spend more money than you make. One reason for the counsel is simple: if we live within our means we will not become a burden to others. Those who take care of themselves financially need never impose on others for financial assistance. Saints who follow the counsel of the Brethren and stay out of debt and live within their means are termed self-reliant.

The principle of self-reliance applies to our emotional resources as well as our financial resources. You can bankrupt yourself emotionally just as surely as you can bankrupt yourself financially if you give more than you possess. If you allow yourself to become discouraged, depressed, or "burned out," that's emotional bankruptcy. If you became emotionally bankrupt, not only would you be unable to give, you could potentially become a burden to others.

Have you ever known someone who worked really hard serving in a particular calling, and then when the person was released he or she became completely inactive in the Church? Do you know people who have had testimonies but who have become offended and left the Church? How often do people who serve valiantly for years suddenly decide they "need a break" and refuse to accept callings?

Folks in these situations are not only in spiritual bankruptcy, but they are also often in emotional bankruptcy. People who take good care of themselves emotionally as well as spiritually can avoid these pitfalls. Members who serve within their means can avoid emotional bankruptcy. They need never become offended, discouraged, "burned out," or resentful.

We can all serve within our means and thus assure that we remain emotionally healthy. Serving within your means requires that you take these steps: first, discover your limitations; second, accept your limitations; third, honor those limitations; and fourth, reveal your limitations.

DISCOVER YOUR LIMITATIONS

Your wonderful body will tell you when you are serving beyond your ability to bear. Your body will even tell you what activities in your life are causing the most stress. Pay attention to your body's signals. When you feel pain, fatigue, or irritability that seem unreasonable, consider the possibility that you are over-stressed. Perhaps you are serving beyond your capacity. Members of the Church have shared with me the following symptoms they experience when they recognize they are feeling too much stress:

- lack of patience (becoming short-tempered with family members)
- lack of energy (finding it hard to drag yourself out of bed in the morning)
- back pain
- neck pain
- frequent and excessively painful headaches
- sore throat that is not viral or bacterial
- gastrointestinal discomfort (ulcers, diarrhea, reflux)

- lowered immune response (the tendency to catch every virus that floats by)
- insomnia
- chronic cold sores and acne

Such symptoms, whether instigated by stress or exacerbated by stress, are the body's warning signs to slow down.

When I was younger I didn't think I had limitations until a painful lesson taught me that I did. One year our ward planned a temple trip to the Atlanta Temple, a six- or seven-hour drive from our home in Jacksonville. We met at the chapel late on a Thursday night, and we drove until morning, arriving at the temple just in time for it to open. Upon arriving at the temple on Friday morning, we began going through back-to-back endowment sessions. Most of our party stopped for lunch and ate in the temple cafeteria, then attended sessions again after lunch. I didn't get to attend the temple very often because of my small children at home, so I decided that as long as I was there I was going to get in as many sessions as I possibly could. I skipped lunch and squeezed in another session. The rest of our party ended their day around 7 P.M., but again, as long as the temple was still open, I decided I would go through a few more sessions. All in all, I completed seven endowment sessions that day. On the way back to our hotel that night I stopped at Hardee's and ate a hamburger, then I fell into bed exhausted and didn't move the whole night (despite the fact that I was sleeping on a hotel bed!).

The next morning we got up early to complete some more sessions, and I felt awful. I felt nauseated and weak. I must have looked awful too, because while I was waiting for an endowment session to begin on Saturday morning, a kindly temple worker approached me and asked if I was well. I admitted I didn't feel very well but insisted I was able enough to complete the session.

Around noon our party piled into the bishop's motor home and returned to Jacksonville. I felt even worse on the way back. By Saturday evening I was doubled over in pain. For the first time in my life I begged my husband for a blessing. The priesthood blessing enabled me to make it through the weekend, and on Monday morning I went to the doctor.

An upper GI series of tests revealed that I had a hiatal hernia. Eating a hamburger with raw onions and sleeping the whole night lying on my stomach had enraged my esophagus. I received all kinds of medication and instructions, including "Never eat right before bed" and "Never sleep on your stomach."

This experience taught me that I was not superwoman. I needed breaks just like other mortals on this planet. I needed to pace myself and give my body a chance to recuperate in order to continue functioning. If I had performed fewer endowment sessions and eaten dinner at a regular hour, I would not had to sleep on a full stomach. If I hadn't been quite so exhausted, I would not have lain in the same position all night, allowing that raw onion to erode my esophagus. I might have spared myself a lot of pain had I accepted my limitations and served at a moderate level rather than working at a breakneck, record-setting pace.

Discovering your limitations and accepting your limitations may take some experimenting as you push yourself and learn how far you can go before "hitting the wall." Once you know your limitations, you need to accept those limitations and resist the temptation to push yourself beyond your capacity. Pushing beyond your capacity can thwart your ability to serve at any level.

ACCEPT YOUR LIMITATIONS

Even when you know you'll pay dearly if you respond positively to someone's request for help, do you still find it difficult to be anything other than helpful? A high priest in one ward learned a great lesson about this. He offered to help one of the brothers in his high priests group build up a retaining wall that kept the brother's property from sliding into the river it bordered. On a Saturday morning several brethren met at the river property, where a load of broken concrete had been delivered. The brethren were to pick up the blocks of concrete and place them on this retaining wall, so at high tide the property would not flood. A very enthusiastic and dedicated high priest, who was a little too old to be lifting heavy concrete blocks, threw out his back at this work party. He became the ward's next service project.

The same principle applies to the father in the delivery room who can't stand the sight of blood and faints on the hospital floor. He disrupts more than he helps. People who push themselves beyond their limits can become a burden to a ward rather than an asset.

A Relief Society teacher in one ward volunteered to help the Relief Society president move boxes into her new home. However, the next day her muscles were so sore from moving boxes the teacher did not attend church and failed to present her lesson. Such examples demonstrate the necessity of serving within your means. Unless you recognize, accept, and honor your limitations, you could become one of those people who needs a casserole brought into the home.

The story of the ill-fated 1996 expedition to Mount Everest, which took the lives of nine climbers, teaches us tremendous lessons in accepting personal limits. Two of the climbers who lost their lives in the Everest disaster were experienced guides. One seems to have lost his life because he overestimated his abilities. Scott Fischer had boasted that "experience is overrated" on Everest. "We've got the big E figured out, we've got it totally wired," Fischer said. "These days, I'm telling you, we've built a yellow brick road to the summit." With this nonchalant attitude, Fischer enticed some climbers onto his team who, like their guide, did not acknowledge their own limitations. Then Fischer expended so much energy rescuing these clients and escorting them from upper camps (26,000 feet) to base camp (21,300 feet) that after he resumed the climb and reached the summit, he did not have enough energy of his own to descend the mountain. At 27,200 feet he died (see Jon Krakauer, *Into Thin Air,* New York: Villard Books, 1997).

You may have legitimately earned the reputation for being your ward's Wonder Woman or Superman. People sing your praises because you are so capable, so dependable. "Give an assignment to Sister Jones, and you know she'll do a bang-up job."

Turning down an assignment can be very difficult when doing so threatens your very identity. Those who thrive on the praise and admiration of others may find it exceptionally difficult to turn down an assignment. They may ask themselves, "Who am I if I am not infinitely helpful and capable?"

The truth is, however, that unless you pace yourself, you compromise your ability to perform to the level you might, had you not overextended yourself.

HONOR YOUR LIMITATIONS

A little-known character in the Book of Mormon teaches us a big lesson about honoring our limitations. In Alma chapter 50, Nephihah, the second chief judge of the Nephites, dies. Verses 37 and 38 teach us two things about Nephihah. One, he filled the judgment seat with perfect uprightness before God. Two, he had refused to take possession of the sacred records. I don't know why

Nephihah refused to take possession of the records, but apparently doing so did not make him a wicked person. He fulfilled the judgment seat with perfect uprightness, even though he refused to keep the sacred records. He gave what he could but also acknowledged his limitations.

We learn from Nephihah that we are not evil people simply because we have limitations. We need not be ashamed of our limitations nor deny ourselves the rest we require.

REVEAL YOUR LIMITATIONS

Some people are embarrassed that they have limitations. They feel guilty that they can't do all the things that are asked of them. Rather than accepting their limitations and feeling content with themselves, even though they have limitations, they feel they have to apologize for their limitations. Do you find that whenever you have to tell someone "no" you generally include an explanation for your answer? You may say something meek like, "I'd love to but I can't, because . . ." Notice that when you say, "I can't" (as if you have no agency), the "I can't" is usually followed by a reason: "because I have to work/travel/baby-sit/study." Notice that you find it easier to say no when you have something else to do. It is difficult to simply say no without an excuse, legitimate or lame.

A devoted Church servant need not manufacture an excuse for saying no. Saints who are anxiously engaged in a good cause always have something else beckoning. And if you are anxiously engaged in good works, that something else is always good. Whenever you say no to one good choice, you are inevitably saying yes to another good choice. "No" never means, "No, I'm just going to sit around and waste time." "No" inevitably means, "I choose to spend my time and energy doing something else of good report." Think of yourself not as saying no to one person but as saying yes to someone else. Even when you plan to stay home and take a hot bubble bath, you are saying yes to yourself and your need to recuperate.

A couple came to my office seeking help with their marriage after an enormous fight. The wife worked at home as a draftsman, drawing plans for houses and apartment buildings. One Friday evening a builder had come over to pick up some plans she had drawn and had found some errors he wanted changed. The builder arrived around five o'clock and stayed and stayed. At 7:00 P.M. the builder was still hanging around the house. The husband was furious because the builder was taking up all of their family time on a Friday night. About an hour into the builder's visit the husband started making snide and even rude comments. He embarrassed the wife in front of the builder, so she was angry with the husband for making such a fool of himself and of her.

In our counseling session the wife admitted that she has a terrible time saying no. She could not possibly tell the builder to go away and come back on Monday.

"I think I get it," I told the wife. "You said yes to the builder, but in saying yes to the builder, you were saying no to your husband."

"You're right!" she exclaimed. "I couldn't say yes to both of them, but instead of saying yes to my husband, I said yes to the builder."

She immediately turned to her husband. "I'm sorry," she said, as sincerely as I've ever heard a person apologize. "I care a lot more about you than about him. I should have said yes to you."

This burst of humility prompted the husband to respond with an equally appropriate apology of his own. He realized that embarrassing his wife in front of her client wasn't the most effective way to persuade her to spend the evening with him.

WHEN YOU SAY NO TO:	YOU MAY ACTUALLY BE SAYING YES TO:
working in the family history center	tending your grandchildren
the service project on Saturday	your son's baseball game
your beauty sleep	the temple trip
your daughter's soccer game	your hair appointment
your boss who wants you to work late	your spouse who wants you to go on a date

You may want to make a list of your own that demonstrates that even if you say no you are still anxiously engaged in good works. Think of the last time you said no. Record the event in the column on the left. Now think of what you chose to say yes to instead. Record that incident in the right-hand column.

Now that you are supporting your spouse in a demanding calling you may be saying no to a number of volunteer opportunities, and yes to keeping the household running smoothly.

Perhaps you can't think of a time you actually said no. Instead, think of a time you said yes even though you didn't want to. Now recall what you could have done instead. The thing you would have preferred doing is the invitation you passed up. This is what you said no to.

The point of this exercise is to help you recognize that when a devoted Church leader says no, that does not make him a mean, selfish, inconsiderate person who never serves his fellowman. When you say no to one person, you actually say yes to another. Although the person you told no may be disappointed, the person you told yes will be elated.

By encouraging devoted Church leaders to say no when necessary, I am not for one second suggesting that Latter-day Saints become selfish and stop serving. Service to our fellowman ranks among the most virtuous of virtues. I am encouraging devoted Church servants to say no without feeling guilty, or without feeling the need to explain. There's nothing evil about saying no to obligations that may take away the energy needed to serve in another capacity that is either a higher priority or something only you can do.

Removing the Guesswork

Because you are the only one who knows your limitations, you are the only one who can honor those limitations. You are the one who knows how much energy you have and how far that energy must extend itself in a given time period. You are the only one who knows when to say yes and when to say no, or to whom you can say yes and to whom you must say no. Those who ask your assistance do not know your circumstances. They do not know your capacity to serve.

A rumor circulated for a time that some cities would routinely put their homeless population on a bus for Utah because Latter-day Saints were so generous about taking care of them. I don't know if the rumor is true, but I can see how it got started. Latter-day Saints are famous for saying yes.

A sister in one ward possessed a talent for decorating cakes. The mother of an Eagle Scout asked her if she could borrow an eagle-shaped pan to make a cake for her son's court of honor. Naturally the sister with the pan said yes. Then the mother-of-the-Scout asked if the sister-with-the-pan could perhaps make the cake for the Eagle court. When one cake proved too small, the mother-of-the-Scout asked the sister-with-the-pan to make an extra cake for the court of honor. Of course the sister-with-the-pan said yes, even though she had company in town for her daughter's graduation and was finishing up her own year as a teacher.

Devoted Church leaders, among all people on this earth, must grow comfortable saying no when situations push them beyond their means. You will be asked to serve by folks who are completely unaware of your limitations and may be astounded to discover such limitations exist. Since you're the only one who knows your own limitations, you are the one responsible for keeping yourself healthy so you have the capacity to continue to serve.

A TOLERANCE FOR TRIALS

Admittedly, not all Church servants push themselves to the limits of their endurance and need to be slowed down. Everybody has a different level of stamina, both physical and emotional, when it comes to service. Some members with a low tolerance for trials can become easily overwhelmed and quickly feel incapable of serving.

However, those who receive calls to leadership positions either start with or soon develop a fairly high tolerance for trials and strong backs and thick skin. Some Church leaders have such strong backs and thick skin we wonder if they truly do have limitations.

Joseph Smith, who preached a sermon the morning after he was tarred and feathered and had one of his teeth chipped, represents an individual with a very high tolerance for trials. Brigham Young and Heber C. Kimball, who left on their missions to England while still suffering from the effects of malaria, had a very high tolerance for trials.

Believing, behaving, and serving Saints want desperately to obey Heavenly Father and, in doing so, serve their fellowman. Those with a high tolerance for trials are willing to give and give and give until they have nothing left to give. Such a sacrifice is not helpful to the kingdom. It's okay to give and give, but please stop short of giving until you have nothing *left* to give. Save some energy. This way you will remain useful and won't become a service project yourself.

Shel Silverstein's book *The Giving Tree* tells the story of a tree who always says yes. Can I climb your branches? Yes. Can I sell your apples? Yes. Can I cut down your trunk? Yes. The poor tree has nothing left to give at the end of the story. The tree then offers herself as a seat to sit on. She gives and gives until she has nothing left to give. Now, that's fine and dandy for the boy who sits on the stump, but what about the tree?

Does Heavenly Father want one of his children to sacrifice herself until she becomes a stump, just so another one of his children can see the world? I believe Heavenly Father cares as much about you and your health as he does about the person who may ask you to give beyond your means. You have a responsibility to take good care of you.

The biggest challenge that faces devoted and faithful servants is knowing when to say "when." Even those who rate the highest on a "tolerance for trials" scale eventually reach their limits. Those who are valiant and true will give their last breath to build up the kingdom of God. However, you undoubtedly don't want the next breath you take, or your spouse takes, to be the last. Thus it becomes necessary to serve within your means.

CHAPTER 12

THE OIL IN
YOUR LAMP

DO YOU KNOW CHILDREN WHO BELIEVE THAT moms never get sick? They think it's against "The Plan" for mothers to get sick! Many mothers work hard to live up to this "plan." Moms, it seems, can't afford to get sick. "If I got sick," one mom defends herself, "then who would take care of the kids, the house, the homework, the laundry . . . ?"

Moms who don't often get sick are not just lucky. They take great care not to get sick. They are religious about getting enough sleep. They wash their hands assiduously so they don't contract germs. They close their eyes and turn their heads when someone sneezes so they don't catch a cold (cold germs enter the eyes as frequently as the nose or the mouth). The virus-resistant mom is not trying to be rude, but she truly can't afford to be sick. She feels obligated to take care of herself. She must stay well so she can attend to all her many responsibilities! You may be one of these health-blessed mothers with the same sense of obligation. Were you to get sick, who would assume all your responsibilities?

As a servant of the Lord, staying physically healthy is not your only obligation. In addition to staying physically healthy, you must stay spiritually healthy and emotionally healthy. It's obvious that you can't serve effectively if you are sick in bed. It's easy to see that you can't bear to others a very strong testimony if your testimony is weak. Equally vital is the necessity of maintaining your emotional health. How can you be a resource to others if you are not emotionally healthy yourself? How can you encourage the discouraged, or uplift the downtrodden, if you are dragging your chin on the concrete? In order to effectively serve in the Lord's kingdom, you need to be physically, spiritually, and emotionally healthy. Those who are *willing* to serve will want to stay healthy so they are *able* to serve.

KEEPING YOUR OWN HOUSE IN ORDER

In my practice I used to work with a Latter-day Saint family who prided themselves in assisting others. The wife could spot trouble a mile away, and she was always the first one on the scene to assist the troubled and downtrodden. One time this helpful family fellowshipped a single sister in their ward who, along with her three children, was in danger of being evicted from her unsanitary apartment. The helpful wife spent two days scrubbing and scraping until the apartment was clean enough to pass inspection. In the meantime dirty laundry piled up in her own home, chicken bones collected under her own kitchen table (literally!), and her four elementary-aged schoolchildren were left to watch over themselves. This dear sister was "robbing Peter to pay Paul." Her attempt to assist others left her own family bereft and suffering.

You can make the greatest contribution to the Church and to your community when, first and foremost, you make sure your own house is in order. Once you are certain your own home is in relatively good order, and you still have resources to give or to share, it is appropriate, even mandatory, that you offer service to your fellowman.

Elder Neal A. Maxwell has said, "When, for the moment, we ourselves are not being stretched on a particular cross, we ought to be at the foot of someone else's" ("Endure It Well," *Ensign*, May 1990, 34). We all crave opportunities to serve, but we can't give when we are stretched on our own crosses. We must have the capacity to serve.

This does not mean your own home needs to be perfect before you give. None of us is perfect, and no home stays in perfect order for very long. You only need relative calm in your own life in order to have the capacity to reach out to others. Should your life be filled with storms, or as Elder Maxwell says, should you be stretched out on your own cross, your priority should be to put your own house in order.

The principle of service is a true principle. But so is the principle of self-reliance. You must take care of your own health—spiritual, physical, and emotional—to have the capacity to attend to someone else's health. In the event of the loss of an airplane's cabin pressure, adults are encouraged to place an oxygen mask on their own face before placing a mask on the face of a child. Similarly, you must make sure you are healthy first in order to have the resources to help others.

There is a sequel to the story of the helpful sister who cleaned the unsanitary apartment. Eventually the family with the unsanitary apartment was evicted from that apartment, and they found themselves temporarily homeless. (My helpful client had provided fish instead of teaching the family to fish.) In light of the homelessness of this messy family, my client invited the family of four to come live with her family in their home. For three weeks a house that was built to hold six people held ten people. The homeless family brought their untidy habits to their temporary abode and imposed on my client until she began to tear her hair out—literally. She came into therapy an emotional wreck. It took twice as long to get her back on track as it would have before the homeless family derailed her.

Many of us have been confused by the expression, "Go the extra mile." Many feel that it's not good enough to simply prepare a thoughtful lesson—they must prepare a thoughtful lesson with visual aids and handouts and centerpieces and multi-media. This concept, that we must "go the extra mile," can cause much needless stress.

The misnomer that we are not giving enough unless we "go the extra mile" likely occurred due to the wording of the King James Version of the Sermon on the Mount. Matthew 5:41 reads, "And whosoever shall compel thee to go a mile, go with him twain." This implies that merely responding to a call to serve is insufficient. This implies that one must do more than is asked.

In the Joseph Smith translation of Matthew the same verse reads, "And whosever shall compel thee to go a mile, *go with him a mile;* and whosoever shall compel thee to go with him twain, thou shalt go with him twain" (*Holy Scriptures* [Independence, Mo.: Herald Publishing House, 1991], 890; italics added). The inspired translation does not encourage us to travel a shorter distance. We are still encouraged to travel two miles when called upon; however, it instructs us to respond directly to the call to serve without feeling compelled to invent additional ways to be someone's hero.

The Sermon on the Mount contains a wealth of valuable and inspired doctrine. The counsel to walk a mile, when called upon to walk a mile, and walk two when called upon to walk two, is consistent with the next verse in the sermon, "Give to him that asketh of thee, and from him that would borrow of thee turn not thou away." In these verses our Savior was not teaching us to give more than is required. He was teaching us to give as much as is required. We are asked to give 10 percent of our income as tithing, not 12 percent, not 20 percent. The scripture instructs us to respond to the call as it is issued.

Giving more than is required of us can jeopardize our emotional health. Trying to do more than is asked, and more than is appropriate, can lead to discouragement and burnout. Those of us who diligently walk all the miles that we are asked to walk will still have iron calves! We need not walk until we become emaciated.

THE PARABLE OF THE TEN VIRGINS

The parable of the ten virgins teaches some profound truths about giving more than you have to give. Upon first reading, the parable of the ten virgins is obviously a warning for foolish virgins: those foolish virgins should have brought enough of their own oil to last until the marriage feast. They should have been prepared. The parable provides a warning to all of us to keep sufficient oil in our lamps.

"Then shall the kingdom of heaven be likened unto ten virgins, which took their lamps, and went forth to meet the bridegroom.

"And five of them were wise, and five were foolish.

"They that were foolish took their lamps, and took no oil with them:

"But the wise took oil in their vessels with their lamps.

"While the bridegroom tarried, they all slumbered and slept.

"And at midnight there was a cry made, Behold, the bridegroom cometh; go ye out to meet him.

"Then all those virgins arose, and trimmed their lamps.

"And the foolish said unto the wise, Give us of your oil; for our lamps are gone out.

"But the wise answered, saying, Not so; lest there be not enough for us and you: but go ye rather to them that sell, and buy for yourselves.

"And while they went to buy, the bridegroom came; and they that were ready went in with him to the marriage: and the door was shut.

"Afterward came also the other virgins, saying, Lord, Lord, open to us.

"But he answered and said, Verily I say unto you, I know you not.

"Watch therefore, for ye know neither the day nor the hour wherein the Son of man cometh" (Matthew 25:1–13).

Upon closer examination of the parable, we recognize that the parable provides a warning not only for the foolish virgins. The parable also gives a strong warning to wise virgins. The wise virgins teach us not to give more than we have to give. The wise virgins refused to share their oil lest there not be enough for them. These wise virgins knew the dangers of giving more than they had to give. They didn't want to be left without enough oil to light their own way.

In likening this parable unto ourselves, we learn that those who are wise virgins—those who follow the prophets and prepare for the marriage feast—can run out of oil if they give too much oil away.

Temporal Preparation

The oil in the virgins' lamps can represent many things. On one level, I believe the oil in the lamps represents exactly that—oil. The oil tells us that the wise virgins were prepared temporally. The virgins who brought sufficient oil thought ahead so they wouldn't run out of oil. Likewise, those of us who are permitted entrance into the marriage feast will be those who are temporally prepared.

The prophets continually instruct us to be prepared temporally. Specific counsel from the prophets regarding temporal preparation includes the following:

- live within your means
- stay out of unnecessary debt
- pay your tithing
- keep a year's supply of food
- get an education
- obey the Word of Wisdom (stay physically healthy)

In today's world those who are ill prepared in temporal matters can be likened unto the foolish virgins. They have not obeyed the prophets who have given ample instructions regarding temporal preparation. The foolish virgins in today's world constantly need temporal assistance. And they turn to the wise virgins for help. (This by no means implies that everyone who turns to the Church for help has failed to follow the prophet. In many cases those who use the Church welfare system do so with integrity. They have encountered temporary hardship that was entirely unforeseen: death, disability, accidents, layoff, and so on. This is the very reason the Church welfare system exists.) The chronic takers are those who remind us of foolish virgins. They never seem to have enough oil.

Those of you who are wise virgins and who are approached by foolish virgins for temporal assistance can benefit from the message in the Savior's parable. Wise virgins, prepared virgins, can be in danger of giving too much temporal oil. You can't loan people money unless you already pay your own bills, or you will soon be on the Church's welfare rolls yourself. You can give only so many pints of blood at the local blood drive. If you were to give too much blood, you would be in the hospital yourself. If you are exhausted after three or four nights of pacing the floor with a sick baby, you are in no condition to spend the next night sitting up at the hospital with an ill ward member. The high priest in the previous chapter who lifted concrete blocks until he threw his back out gave more than he had to give.

Limited Spiritual Oil

The wise virgins teach a lesson about spiritual preparation as well. The wise virgins knew they couldn't give away their spiritual oil lest there not be enough left for them to get into the marriage feast.

One of the ways we might give too much spiritual oil is by trying to debate someone who has delved into anti-Mormon literature. It is not likely we can entertain devilish arguments and remain unscathed. It has been said the devil may knock on your door, but you don't have to invite him into the living room for a conversation. Spiritual oil is conserved by closing the door to evil, not by entertaining it.

Perhaps you have known an adolescent or young adult who befriended the "wild" type in hopes of converting them to the gospel. A young woman may fall in love with a young man who does not live the principles of the gospel, claiming that she is going to convert her beloved. In too many cases, the wild young man converts the righteous Latter-day Saint instead. She who had a strong testimony loses it and lives the lifestyle of the young man whom she sought to convert. This is an example of giving too much spiritual oil.

Limited Emotional Oil

Just as we can give too much temporal oil and be left without lights in our own homes, and we can give too much spiritual oil and have our testimonies ravaged by enemies of the Savior, we can also give too much emotional oil.

You can recognize when you are running low on emotional oil when you become discouraged, depressed, angry, resentful, or sad. This is the time to pause and make sure you have not given too much emotional oil and left none for yourself.

How can you discern the ways in which you are giving too much emotional oil? Pay close attention to the moment you begin to experience the negative emotions. Then think about the events that precede your negative emotions. If you said yes when you should have said no, you might feel angry. If you have been taken advantage of, you may feel resentful. Perhaps you agreed to baby-sit for two hours, and you ended up keeping children for four hours. You may have agreed to help bring dinner to a family, and the person who agreed to help you backed out at the last minute and left you to cook the entire meal.

One valiant young father came in for counseling with severe depression. He was a salesman who worked strictly on commission and had not made a sale for two solid months. He was also the Young Men president in his ward and struggled mightily with his calling. He showed up diligently for the Young Men activity each Wednesday, but neither of his counselors ever came. Between twelve and eighteen young men attended the Wednesday night activity, and my client was responsible for all of them. The young men ran wild on Wednesday nights. They did not cooperate with the program he planned, and they actually made fun of their leader at times. He confessed to me that he felt like a complete and utter failure. Between the struggles he was having at work and the struggles he was having in his calling, he had hit rock bottom.

It took several weeks for him to accept his limitations. He loved the gospel with all his might and wanted desperately to serve the Lord, but he was drowning in his current position. With time he developed some skills for dealing with rambunctious adolescents. He also mustered the courage to ask for some reliable help in the Young Men organization, and eventually he felt his head peek above water. This Young Men president learned to swim by admitting he was drowning. He had to accept his limitations, seek appropriate help, and develop the skills to meet the challenges he faced before he could return to the ranks of the givers.

STAYING EMOTIONALLY HEALTHY

Think about how hard you work to keep yourself from becoming physically sick. You try to get plenty of sleep, eat healthy food, exercise, drink lots of water, and wash your hands to avoid catching a virus. You have too many people counting on you. You can't afford to get sick.

Saints can't afford to get sick of service either. If one of us goes on the sick list (or the inactive or less-active list), then that leaves the rest of us to take care of his or her responsibilities. When one person gets sick, the well folks have an even greater burden. They have to take care of all those people who were previously sick, and now they have to take care of a new patient who allowed himself to become burned out. Church leaders cannot afford to push themselves beyond their ability to bear. The kingdom of God cannot afford for any one of us to take on a load too heavy for our shoulders. We can't afford for anyone to carry an unjustly heavy burden, because we can't afford to lose one single valiant servant to overwork, exhaustion, or burnout. Therefore, it is as important that we keep ourselves emotionally healthy as it is that we keep ourselves physically healthy.

The wise virgins in the parable of the ten virgins teach us a very valuable message: don't give more than you can bear to give. Keep enough oil to meet your own spiritual, temporal, and emotional needs. Accept your limitations. Acknowledge your strengths and your weaknesses. Serving within your means is not selfish; it is wise.

DIFFERENT CAPACITIES TO SERVE

You need never be ashamed to serve within your means. I know two sisters who are visiting teaching companions who have very different capabilities. One of the women suffers from fibromyalgia. She sleeps poorly at night and aches most of the day. The other must have pioneer blood running thick through her veins because she books her schedule from sunrise to sunset and barely stops for breath. Frequently the fibromyalgia victim expresses embarrassment because she can't keep the same pace of service as her visiting teaching companion. The energetic companion always reassures her friend: "There is no shame in serving within your means."

Some people have a whole bunch of money and some have very little money. The person with the wads of money isn't a better person than the one with less money. The person with the wads of riches can still spend too much money and contract too much debt, while the person with less money may know how to live within his means. Those who want to be obedient don't worry about making millions of dollars; they worry about living within their means. The poor person who lives within his means is just as obedient as the rich person who lives within his means.

Just as some people have more money than others, some people have more time and energy than others. A grandmother once joked about this subject with her granddaughter. The family had just returned from a busy day at an amusement park and a nice evening at a dinner theater. The granddaughter walked into the house at ten o'clock at night and whipped up a batch of home-made chocolate chip cookies for the family to enjoy with a glass of cold milk before they went to bed. The grandmother lamented that if she wants to bake a batch of homemade chocolate chip cookies, she puts it on her calendar, and that's the only thing she plans for the entire day. The granddaughter embraced her grand-mother and leaned over to whisper in her ear, "Grandma, your cookies will taste just as delicious on the day you bake as these did this evening. Please invite me over to have some!"

Our Father in Heaven does not value one individual more than another simply because one's capacity to serve is greater. Our Heavenly Father values the fact that we are giving the best we have to give. In the parable of the talents, the only slothful ser-vant was the one who buried his talent. The lord in the parable approved of both the man who was given two talents and doubled them *and* the man who was given five talents and doubled them (see Matthew 25:14–30).

There will be times when you give as much as you possibly can—without falling over in utter exhaustion—and the still find that the work is not completed. You may even feel as if you didn't do enough. But when you have given what you are capable of giving, you have given enough. You will not be judged by what percent of the job you completed but by what percent of effort you put forth. When you have given to your capacity, the job still may not be done, but you are. You will have given as much as you can possibly give and still have enough oil for yourself. You will have given as much as you possibly can manage to give and still function in your primary role as a husband or wife, a mom or a dad.

PART THREE

TAKING CARE OF
THE CHILDREN

CHAPTER 13

PRESSURE TO SET
AN EXAMPLE

DAYS AFTER MY HUSBAND WAS CALLED TO SERVE AS bishop we attended a wedding reception at a very old and prestigious country club on the St. Johns River. Ivy-coated brick surrounded a grand entrance. Inside, wall-to-wall windows overlooked sailboats and yachts on the river below.

The buffet that evening consisted of shrimp from the river we admired, along with crab and lobster from the nearby Atlantic. But the table that caught my eye held strawberries, chocolates, and whipped cream. A spray of spoons dipped in chocolate surrounded the display. Signs labeled the spoons "mint," "orange," and "amaretto" for those who wanted to stir a little flavor into their coffee.

I was just about to stick a spoon in my mouth and suck it like a lollipop when the mother of the bride appeared. "JeaNette, come here," she whispered. I took one longing glance across my shoulder at the chocolate spoons as she dragged me away.

I soon stood in front of one of the most wealthy men in our

town. His name appeared in the newspaper constantly, and his biography was currently on bookstore shelves. But he knew little or nothing about Latter-day Saints.

"Mr. Phelps," Christina began, "meet our bishop's wife."

Bishop's wife? My eyes darted to hers and I squinted to make sure this was my friend talking. *Just yesterday we flipped a coin for the last extra-small sweater on the clothing store sale rack. We've shared running shoes and even swimsuits. Don't you want to introduce me as . . . an old friend?*

Certainly it would have been a fine compliment to be introduced as a friend. However, I realized that evening that my husband was not the only one who had recently assumed a new role. Even for my friends, I had assumed a new role too. People would be looking at me differently now. *Now, about those chocolate spoons.*

Whether we like it or not, Church leaders and their families are often watched very carefully. Members looking for an example will observe the way their leaders act, dress, perform in their callings, and especially how they raise their children. Parents may put intense pressure on themselves, and also on their children, to provide the perfect example.

I was feeling acutely responsible for setting a good example when, one Sabbath morning, my deacon-aged son showed up at church without any shoes. He had on athletic socks, and no shoes at all—not his church shoes, not his sandals, not his sneakers, not his cleats. The church was twenty minutes away from home and if I drove back to get his shoes I would miss sacrament meeting. I cringed as I imagined what people would think of the bishop's son attending church without his shoes: *How unorganized the bishop's wife must be, how scatterbrained! She probably slept too late. Hasn't she heard the song "Saturday is a special day, it's the day we get ready for Sunday . . . "? She should have had her children's clothes all set out the night before.* My face was hot with shame as I sat in the parking lot, pondering my dilemma. I wanted to turn around and drive home and let people guess why I missed sacrament meeting rather than watch my stocking-clad son patter from class to class.

As I sat there, I pondered a silent prayer and felt impressed that I should go to sacrament meeting. I felt that it was more important that I renew my covenants and feel the spirit of the meeting—and that my children see that it was more important for me to renew my covenants and feel the spirit of the meeting— than for them all to appear perfectly starched and pressed that morning.

So Tanner walked to all his meetings that day in stocking feet. (However, he did not pass the sacrament in his socks.)

One of the most stressful requirements of supporting a spouse in a leadership position is dealing with the knowledge that your family will be subjected to a bit of scrutiny. You've heard the old saying, "Folks on a pedestal have to watch their step!" The top of a pedestal is a pretty scary place to stand. Individuals in such a spot may feel paralyzed or unable to breathe, fearing one false move could topple them to the ground.

Even before my husband became a bishop I felt weighed down by the responsibility of setting a good example. As a child I felt keenly the eyes of my seven younger siblings upon me. As an adult, living in communities where the only thing people know about our church is what I show them, I have felt obligated to provide my neighbors with a positive impression of the Church. I often fantasized about the convenience of being invisible just in case I, or one of my children, did something that would cause us to fall off somebody's pedestal.

Once I wrote an article for the *New Era* called "The Shirt I Was Afraid to Wear." In the article I described a BYU T-shirt that stayed clean and pressed in my bottom drawer because I was afraid that if I wore the shirt in public, and then were to act in a way unbecoming a Latter-day Saint, such as cutting someone off in traffic or showing impatience with a slow sales clerk, I would reflect poorly on the Church.

What I really wanted to wear, instead of a BYU T-shirt, was a T-shirt that read, "Don't follow me, I'm lost too." That, however, would definitely be hiding my light under a bushel (see *New Era*, February 1993, 26).

Even though you might prefer to protect yourself from public scrutiny by hiding your light under a bushel, as a Latter-day Saint, and as a leader among the Latter-day Saints, you have a wonderful opportunity to influence others for good. When so many need good examples, it would be a shame to completely give up the opportunity to inspire others to live a more Christlike life. President Gordon B. Hinckley has encouraged us to rise to the occasion and be lights unto the world.

"As His followers, we cannot do a mean or shoddy or ungracious thing without tarnishing His image. Nor can we do a good and gracious and generous act without burnishing more brightly the symbol of Him whose name we have taken upon ourselves.

"Our lives must become a symbol of meaningful expression, the symbol of our declaration of our testimony of the living Christ, the Eternal Son of the living God" ("Our One Bright Hope," *Ensign,* April 1994, 2).

Years of pondering this dilemma have helped me resolve my conflict between being a light unto the world and my fear that I, or one of my children, might fall off a pedestal.

DON'T SWEAT THE SMALL STUFF

You may have seen the motivational poster that reads, "Don't sweat the small stuff . . . " and then at the bottom it adds, "It's all small stuff." Obviously, the statement, "It's all small stuff," is not true. It's not all small stuff. There are some commandments that are huge. Our salvation depends on our obedience to specific, vital commandments.

"It is our privilege to consecrate our time, talents, and means to build up his kingdom," Elder Bruce R. McConkie declared. "We are called upon to sacrifice, in one degree or another, for the furtherance of his work. Obedience is essential to salvation; so, also, is service; and so, also, are consecration and sacrifice" ("Obedience, Consecration, and Sacrifice," *Ensign,* May 1975, 50).

Of course we want to pay attention to the commandments of our Heavenly Father in order to return to him. We can't even consider disregarding them. We must be vigilant about the things that truly matter.

I do, however, agree with the first half of the poster: "Don't sweat the small stuff." Chieko Okazaki's "lighten up" concept encourages us not to sweat the small stuff. The tricky task, the challenge we all face, is determining what is small stuff and what isn't.

A young mother visited my office once because her five-year-old daughter was out of control. The mother recognized that she was very hard on this daughter. She monitored everything from what the child ate to what she wore to how she kept her room to what she said to the adults she met. The child was defiant in all areas, causing the mother much distress. After a couple of sessions, the mother realized that she wasn't nearly as concerned about her daughter's eating habits, her dress, or her room as she was about her daughter's manners when she met an adult. The mother determined to lighten up a bit in other areas and to focus exclusively on how the child responded when she met an adult.

Personally, I thought the mother was expecting too much to ask a five-year-old to look adults in the eye, and to speak to them articulately and in complete sentences. I might have focused more on eating habits or dress if it were my child, and allowed the little girl to relax around adults. However, that was not my decision to make. To this mother, the way her child greeted adults was the most critical behavior her child could manifest. The mother enforced what she considered the "big" stuff and decided not to sweat the small stuff, and the child thrived. Her behavior improved dramatically in all areas.

Your family may have its own list of big stuff *vs.* small stuff. That's perfectly okay. With the guidance of the scriptures and the prophets as well as the inspiration of the Holy Ghost, you will determine where you want to expend your time and energy, and what you can let slide.

In our home we have determined that what you wear on the Sabbath day is important, but not nearly as important as where you are on the Sabbath day. We have determined that the content of our family home evenings is important, but not nearly as important as the fact that we have family home evenings. We have determined that having daily family prayer is far more important then where we have it, when we have it, who says it, or what is said. We have determined that showing up at a ward social is more important than what we bring. We have determined that going visiting teaching and home teaching is more important than how long we stay or what goodies we leave.

Relaxing in a few areas that we deem possible to relax in has helped lighten our family's load. Our hardworking fellow Saints can feel that they are doing pretty darn good if they attend to the big stuff, and there is no need sweat the small stuff.

Your own list of big stuff *vs.* small stuff might not look like your neighbor's list. The important point is that you allow yourself some latitude in areas that are not of eternal significance. The personal load that you carry as leaders in the Church and the load you place on your children's backs can evaporate ounce by ounce when you relax and let the small stuff float away so you can focus primarily on the areas upon which your salvation depends.

DEFLECTING CRITICISM

Should Church leaders receive criticism from the folks who have placed them on a pedestal, they can be reassured that most of the time they won't even have done anything wrong. Usually, when someone criticizes the behavior of a Church leader or the leader's family, the critics are most often concerned about the small stuff.

People will simply have a different opinion than you do as to how a bishop's wife or other Church leader should behave. Because they have one opinion, and you another, does not make them right and you wrong. It makes you each different. You can view such criticism as merely a difference of opinion rather than a condemnation. When you encounter folks who are extremely opinionated, their conviction may cause you to doubt yourself. But if you allow the Holy Ghost to guide your life, then as confident as they appear, you can still be more certain that you are making decisions that are consistent with the Father's will.

One time while my husband was serving as bishop, the Cub Scout leaders got into a huge tiff. Angry words were exchanged and accusations flung about. To rid the organization of the ugly atmosphere of contention, my husband released all the leaders at once. The next Wednesday he ran the den meeting himself. He came straight from work in his tie and wing tips without a Scout manual or equipment. To entertain the boys he took off his shoes and loosened his tie and engaged the boys in a lively game of Simon Says. One of the women, who had recently been released from her position as den leader, sat at the back of the cultural hall and watched him. She repeated resentful remarks to all who would listen: "Look at the bishop making a fool of himself. That's what happens when you come unprepared."

Naturally her remarks got back to the bishop, and even though the criticism was unwarranted and inappropriate, he came home that night as deflated as I've ever seen him. He dropped onto the sofa next to me and told me what had transpired. With all the love I could show, I tried to comfort him. The image of Michelangelo's *Pieta* filled my mind, and I thought I knew a fraction of what it was like to be Mary.

A classic talk by Elder Dallin H. Oaks teaches us that "criticism is particularly objectionable when it is directed toward Church authorities, general or local. Jude condemns those who 'speak evil of dignities.' (Jude 1:8.) Evil speaking of the Lord's anointed is in a class by itself. It is one thing to depreciate a person who exercises corporate power or even government power. It is quite another thing to criticize or depreciate a person for the performance of an office to which he or she has been called of God. It does not matter that the criticism is true. As Elder George F. Richards, President of the Council of the Twelve, said in a conference address in April 1947, 'When we say anything bad about the leaders of the Church, whether true or false, we tend to impair their influence and their usefulness and are thus working against the Lord and his cause.' (In Conference Report, Apr. 1947, p. 24.)" ("Criticism," *Ensign,* February 1987, 68).

Not only do critics of Church leaders enjoy making a big deal of small stuff—stuff that has no eternal significance—critics frequently know very little about the situation they choose to criticize. They are quite often grossly misinformed or underinformed, and they have no capacity to make an accurate assessment of the situation they criticize.

Elder Oaks continues, "The counsel against speaking evil of Church leaders is not so much for the benefit of the leaders as it is for the spiritual well-being of members who are prone to murmur and find fault" (ibid., 68).

Consider the experience of Alma the Younger who went about persecuting the Church. We all know how he felt when he discovered how wrong he had been:

"I was racked with eternal torment, for my soul was harrowed up to the greatest degree and racked with all my sins.

"Yea, I did remember all my sins and iniquities, for which I was tormented with the pains of hell; yea, I saw that I had rebelled against my God, and that I had not kept his holy commandments. . . .

"Oh, thought I, that I could be banished and become extinct both soul and body, that I might not be brought to stand in the presence of my God, to be judged of my deeds" (Alma 36:12–13, 15).

One who criticizes Church leaders may very well find that he or she is uninformed, underinformed, or misinformed, and that the criticism was entirely unwarranted. One can only imagine the anguish they will feel when they come to themselves and recognize the error of their ways.

Granted, there will be times when Church leaders goof in a major way. We will make big mistakes, not like forgetting our Sunday shoes. President Thomas S. Monson has told of a time that a bishop forgot to attend the funeral of a member's small child:

"I am acquainted with a family which came to America from Germany. The English language was difficult for them. They had but little by way of means, but each was blessed with the will to work and with a love of God.

"Their third child was born, lived but two months, and then died. Father was a cabinetmaker and fashioned a beautiful casket for the body of his precious child. The day of the funeral was gloomy, thus reflecting the sadness they felt in their loss. As the family walked to the chapel, with Father carrying the tiny casket, a small number of friends had gathered. However, the chapel door was locked. The busy bishop had forgotten the funeral. Attempts to reach him were futile. Not knowing what to do, the father placed the casket under his arm and, with his family beside him, carried it home, walking in a drenching rain" ("Hidden Wedges," *Ensign,* May 2002, 18).

That's a pretty big goof, but it does not make the bishop a sinner. It is obvious that Church leaders are less than perfect, and it is inevitable that they will sometimes goof up. Church leaders who goof up are not sinners, they are mortals, subject to memory loss and fatigue and poor judgment and all the other limitations of our second estate.

On occasion, a Church leader will actually commit a sin, and practically everybody will know about it because of his or her visible position. Should such a tragedy occur, a Church leader has the opportunity to apply the Atonement in his life and can provide an excellent example of the principle of repentance.

REVEALING OUR HUMANITY

My struggle with Sunday mornings manifested itself yet another time while my husband was serving as bishop. Just as we pulled into the parking lot at church one morning, I noticed my priest-aged son had not pressed his pants.

"You forgot to iron your pants!" I exclaimed as I glanced over at my ruddy-cheeked sixteen-year-old.

"I didn't forget," my son replied. "I ironed them just a minute ago."

"Look!" I exclaimed.

He glanced down at his legs and dismay crossed his face. "Oh, man . . . I only ironed one leg."

Everyone in the car began to laugh and we could barely suppress our snickers even as we entered the chapel. My son was certain his friends would laugh as hard as his siblings did. He was right. But it turned out the members were laughing *with* Spencer, not *at* him.

The incident lightened many a load that day. Several ward members expressed relief in discovering the bishop's family was not perfect. They felt relieved because it became apparent that we all struggle with our Sunday schedules and there was plenty of room in our building for those who did not glide effortlessly through the day.

Upon discovering how relieved our ward members became once they saw evidence that the bishop's family was not the model of perfection, I gulped down my fear and allowed ward members to glance into our lives and see evidence that we're human and we have our limitations. When people came over for family home evening, I wrung my hands together in order to resist the temptation to polish the doorknobs with my shirt tail. Committed not to hide behind an array of posters and puppets and costumes and flannel boards when I taught the family home evening lesson, I sometimes felt like hyperventilating. However, a few deep breaths helped me make it to dessert, which was deliberately simple and took little time to prepare. The experiment took a lot of courage, but I wanted to show my friends that it is okay to focus on what really matters and accept that it is not a sin to fall a tad short in areas of lesser significance.

In the long run, I discovered that revealing my humanity drew more affection than criticism, particularly from those who were struggling, just as I was, to do their very best.

One family revealed that any time one of their children climbs in the car without his shoes they tease the child, "Oh, you're pulling a Tanner, are you?" in memory of the day Tanner attended church without his shoes.

SUPPORT FROM LIKE-MINDED SAINTS

On more than one occasion I have made difficult decisions that drew chunks of criticism from the world. The sneers of the world will come into the lives of Saints who live the gospel. As Latter-day Saints we may be criticized because we have a lot of children, we may be criticized because mothers stay home, we may be criticized because we spend so much time serving at church, we may be criticized because we won't participate in Sunday recreational activities, we may be criticized because we shun certain media, we may be criticized because our shorts are so long or because we don't work in our yards on Sunday, and so on and so on. The world is full of critics that may not approve of the choices we each make. You may even encounter some of those critics right in your own congregation, even among your fellow Latter-day Saints.

In addition to scattered criticism, however, you will also receive overwhelming support from those who appreciate your choice to do what you believe is right.

Even though many eyes may be upon you, not all of those

eyes will be critical of you. When you are obeying promptings of the Spirit and following the commandments of our Heavenly Father, those who listen to the same Spirit and also follow the commandments will applaud your decisions. You can take comfort from the support of like-minded Saints.

I lived in Connecticut in the early 1980s when the campaign for women's rights was in full swing. July of 1982 was the deadline to ratify the ERA amendment and women who failed to use their education and "wasted" their intelligence staying home and rearing children were scorned by many of their sisters. At the time I had one child in a stroller and one on the way. Every day my firstborn and I would walk to the town green, taking dry bread to feed the ducks and hoping to find other young mothers who were also walking their toddlers on the green. I hoped that our children might play together and we could form a friendship. Whenever I saw a new face sitting on the bench next to the duck pond I introduced myself. Day after day I met women on the green. However, I never met the mothers of the other toddlers. The women I met were not the mothers, but the nannies. The mothers were on a train, commuting to their Manhattan offices. It was a difficult time in history and a difficult place in the country to be a stay-at-home mother. I felt like five-dollar-an-hour hired help. I thought my college degree was wasted.

Fortunately, I found camaraderie among the sisters of Zion. Although we had to travel quite a distance to get together, I found other young mothers in our ward who had also chosen to stay home with their children. We began to exercise together and take our children on outings, and I felt a little less isolated due to the support of my Latter-day Saint sisters.

Similar camaraderie existed between the young women in the San Francisco Bay Area who together approached the fashion designers at a major department store and convinced them to create a line of prom dresses that adhered to the Church's standards of modesty. Youth who band together and make exciting plans for prom that do not include immorality or drinking know what it is like to feel supported by like-minded friends.

PERFORMING FOR AN AUDIENCE OF ONE

The voices of the critics, no matter how incessant or how whiney, cannot compare in impact to the voice of God, spoken with thunder throughout the ages. Neither can the voices of the critics compare to the whisperings of the Holy Ghost, penetrating our individual souls. I almost consider it a compliment when someone criticizes me for not being of the world because it reminds me whose side I have chosen. At least it's obvious.

When the promptings of the Holy Ghost guide your life, you will have no reason to heed the promptings of your fellowmen. The things you do will remain the same whether your fellowmen are watching with approval or with criticism.

If you are *tempted* to change your behavior because somebody is watching, you may be giving more weight to the opinion of others than to the Holy Ghost. Doing so can weaken the effect of the Holy Ghost in your life.

President Ezra Taft Benson taught a most profound truth: "The proud stand more in fear of men's judgment than of God's judgment" ("Beware of Pride," *Ensign,* May 1989, 5).

Saints who reach the point where they always make decisions according to the will of Heavenly Father can dismiss the judgments of the world as summarily as they might dismiss a pop-up ad on the Internet.

CHAPTER 14

PRESSURE TO RAISE PERFECT CHILDREN

RECENTLY I VISITED A STAKE WHERE A NEW STAKE president had just been called to serve. His son's first question upon learning about the call was, "So Dad, do I have to be good all the time now?"

Children of Church leaders can feel a great deal of pressure to set a good example when their parents serve in leadership positions. And it goes without saying that when you are a Church leader, your children's behavior may be scrutinized. Of all the things you pressure yourself to do, the pressure to have your children set an outstanding example may be among the most stressful.

It's daunting to imagine that your behavior, or that of your children, can influence others so significantly. Some leaders may feel that one false move can cause irreparable damage to both their own children and those of other parents. Some might seriously fear that if they make a wrong decision regarding their parenting, others might then justify copying them. Such leaders put a great deal of pressure on themselves when they feel responsible for the behavior of their own children *and* all the children who watch their children.

Because parenting is a real challenge, it's natural for members to closely observe the way Church leaders parent. Members may derive their own child-rearing practices based on the child-rearing practices of a Church leader. They may even alter their child-rearing practices based on the way the Church leaders raise their own children.

For example, if a Church leader allows his daughter to go on a date a few weeks before her sixteenth birthday, other LDS parents may think it is okay to follow suit. Parents who witness a Church leader's son with long or disheveled hair may justify similar styles for their own sons.

The obligation to set an example for other parents to follow is only one reason parents pressure themselves to raise exemplary children. Another reason Church leaders pressure themselves to raise exemplary children is because they believe their teachings will be more believable if their own children accept them. Leaders may feel that their children's obedience adds to their own credibility and their children's disobedience takes away from their credibility. Alma the Younger told his son Corianton that because of Corianton's bad example, the people Alma was responsible for teaching would not listen to his words. "Behold, O my son, how great iniquity ye brought upon the Zoramites; for when they saw your conduct they would not believe in my words" (Alma 39:11).

PRESSURE ON THE CHILDREN

Parents who feel this tremendous responsibility to set an example for others may make different parenting decisions than they would if they were not subject to such close scrutiny.

They may put pressure on their children to perform to an exceptionally high standard. They may have far less tolerance for mistakes than they otherwise would. They may expect greater performance in all areas than they would without the leadership title.

Parents with leadership positions may tighten their children's choices to the point that the children are so exact in the way they keep the commandments that there is no way anyone could possibly be led astray by their example. And they may do all this just to make sure no one uses them as an excuse for misbehavior.

The effect this pressure has on children will vary widely according to the individual child.

ACCEPTING THE FISHBOWL CHALLENGE

Plenty of the children raised by Church leaders have accepted the challenge of leadership and set fine examples for their peers. They inspire the other youth of the Church and show them that it is possible to live the commandments and to live a joyful life in the world but not of the world.

These youth may organize wholesome activities for their peers. They may turn down invitations to social events that are inappropriate. They may reach out and fellowship less-active youth. These youth are not afraid to speak up at firesides or youth conferences and to share their convictions. They live the gospel with thorough obedience. They accept the responsibility of leadership and live the commandments with precision and exactness.

FLEEING THE FISHBOWL CHALLENGE

Other children may resent the higher expectations placed upon them, and they may rebel and make choices that are the opposite of those their parents encourage. The responsibility to set an example for other youth may cause a leader's child to feel overwhelmed.

Rather than rise to the occasion and perform at an even higher level than they would if their parents were not Church leaders, such children may run away from the challenge and they may run in the opposite direction from their parents.

Several years ago a mother approached me, concerned about her son. The parents called this child their "golden boy" because they claimed he was perfect in every way. They claimed he had never given them a day of trouble in his life. Then her husband was called to serve in the stake presidency, and the boy started using marijuana. Upon being questioned about his decision, the boy responded that he was "tired of being the golden boy."

Another sister stood at the pulpit to bear her testimony after fifteen years of being less active in the Church. "I was one of those bishops' brats," she said. "My brothers and sisters and I were the worst kids in the ward."

I had never heard this expression before, and it alarmed me. It implied that there were enough disobedient children of Church leaders that they were their own demographic, and on top of that they actually had a *label*.

No More Bishops' Brats

We have such a wonderful opportunity to influence others for good when all eyes are upon us that it would be a shame to completely give up the opportunity to inspire others to live a more Christlike life. However, at the same time, we don't want our children to feel so overburdened by responsibility that they flee from it.

An easy solution would be to encourage everybody to make

their own parenting decisions and stop looking to Church leaders for an example. However, tremendous good can come from leaders who are willing to accept the responsibility to set an example for others. Youth who set a good example for their peers make it infinitely easier for their peers to live the gospel.

We teach our children in Primary that they are responsible for setting a good example for their peers. Verse two in the Primary song "The Things I Do" says,

> The people in my neighborhood
> Will judge the gospel bad or good
> By how I act at work and play,
> And not just on the Sabbath day.
> *(Children's Songbook,* 170)

I have struggled with this dilemma in my own home. I want my children to set a good example for their peers, but I don't want to put so much pressure on them that they feel incapable of living up to my expectations and they give up.

As I pondered this situation, I remembered a principle I learned in graduate school. We were studying test anxiety, and we learned that test performance is closely related to anxiety. The studies showed that when students experienced low levels of anxiety while taking tests, it led to poor performance, and high anxiety while taking tests also led to poor performance. The highest scores on the tests were earned by the students experiencing moderate anxiety.

I believe that putting too much pressure on our youth can have a counterproductive effect, much like putting too much pressure on oneself when taking a test. I believe that a moderate approach to parenting must exist within which our children can comfortably perform.

Highly concerned that my own children not become so over-whelmed with the responsibility of setting an example that they stopped trying, I have spent a great deal of effort helping them deal with "living in a fishbowl." The following ideas may help your children see the importance of obedience, while taking the edge off their anxiety.

We Are Responsible for Our Own Salvation

I believe it is unnecessary to put our children on a pedestal and require that they perform flawlessly while everybody watches. Being good because your own salvation depends on it is pressure enough, but believing that others' salvation is dependent on your good behavior may be a burden too heavy for our children to bear.

Diane K. Jennings, the wife of a former bishop, taught her children that they "should be examples of Christian living and make proper choices, not just because they were the bishop's children but because it was right. We reminded ourselves often that they were individuals with free agency; they could be guided and led, but not pushed and forced for the sake of appearance" ("Sustaining, Supporting, and Surviving—As the Wife of a Busy Church Leader," *Ensign,* October 1980, 48).

Even though youth do have a responsibility to set an example, that should not be the primary motivation for the decisions they make. Their primary motivation should be to work out their own salvation.

Each of us has our individual agency, and nobody can justify bad behavior with the excuse, "So-and-so is doing it." Should a person choose to follow my child's example, that is the individual's privilege. But if they choose to copy inappropriate behavior, they personally are responsible for the consequences.

When my children make decisions, I encourage them to ask themselves if they are making a choice that will bring them back to their Heavenly Father, and not to ask themselves who will be watching.

Of course, the natural consequence of making correct choices is that if someone happens to copy your children, they will be copying a good example. However, this need not be the primary motive of a child struggling to make good decisions. If impressing others were the primary motive of a child's decision making, children would begin to put inordinate amounts of effort into sneaking around and misbehaving without people knowing.

Decision making becomes far simpler when children consider their own salvation, not everybody else's. The children feel less pressured, less weighed down, less scrutinized. And they do what's right because they themselves want to be obedient, not because others want them to be obedient.

Children who are struggling to make decisions that will bring about their own salvation can remind themselves of the following truths:

- If the behavior is good, it doesn't matter who is watching (if someone happens to notice, he will always be influenced positively)
- If the behavior is wrong, it's wrong whether anyone is watching or not (regardless of whether anyone notices, the child will still be responsible for his own misbehavior)

The question "Who might be watching me that I don't want to provide a bad example?" should not be the basis of decision making. The question, "Is this behavior conducive to my own salvation?" should be the basis of decision making.

When we guide our children, we can take care not to

motivate them with the question "What will the neighbors think?" but instead motivate with the question "What will Heavenly Father think?" We can instill in our children the fear of God, rather than instilling in them the fear of the neighbors.

Gaining a Perspective on Sacrifice

Sometimes, on the way to church, my children and I play a game they thoroughly enjoy. They tell me their dreams from the night before, and I analyze their dreams for them.

One morning my eldest son shared his dream: Dad (who was the bishop at the time) was walking across the front of the chapel so he could go sit on the stand, when someone sitting on the front row grabbed his suit coat and wouldn't let go. The bishop tugged and pulled and the person still wouldn't let go of his suit coat so he could go sit on the stand.

My son's dream helped me see that the responsibility to set a good example is not the only thing children of Church leaders fear. In this particular dream, it became apparent that my son's perception was that great demands were being placed on his father, demands his father could not avoid. This perception, that a parent's Church service is highly demanding and the parent is somehow "trapped" by the demands, can cause the children in an active LDS family considerable concern. My son is not the only child with this worry.

The fear of service is actually one of the excuses some members of the rising generation give for leaving the Church. I have known several talented, capable couples over the years who, although they both grew up in the Church and one or both served missions and had been reared by parents who fulfilled significant leadership roles, chose inactivity as adults. Concerned about such choices, I have mustered the courage to ask these individuals about their thinking.

Over and over again these capable Saints confess that living the gospel was "too much work." They watched their parents devote so much of their time and talents and energy to Church service that they concluded their parents were deprived of any fun. They concluded that their parents never did anything for themselves or their family because they were always so burdened by Church obligations.

As you and your spouse serve valiantly in the Church, I hope and pray your children never perceive your choice to serve in such an inaccurate and short-sighted manner. While it is true that children will witness many hours of labor in the Lord's behalf, they need never perceive such labor as depriving you of that which you most enjoy. Children who only see the long hours and the hard work their parents devote to the Church only see half the picture. Parents must, absolutely must, make sure their children see the whole picture. This can be done in the following manner.

Debriefing

In order for your children to appreciate the joy of service, they need to learn "the rest of the story." After a service project, or a youth temple trip, or a youth conference, the youth frequently hold testimony meetings wherein they share what they have gained from their experience. Similarly, your children will be greatly blessed not just by watching you serve but also by enjoying a "debriefing" on occasion. They need to hear your testimonies as to why you serve and the blessings that have resulted.

Family home evenings can be ideal debriefing meetings, like a testimony meeting that follows a youth temple trip. At family home evening, your children can see the whole picture, as you declare your faith and describe the joy associated with serving the Lord.

One Mother's Day the priests in a certain ward went around the room and took turns telling their adviser what they loved about their mothers. Some appreciated their mother's luscious lunches, and others were grateful that she always washed their clothes. However, one sixteen-year-old young man said with reverence, "My mother treasures the scriptures. Some day I want to love the scriptures the way my mother loves the scriptures."

This mother communicated so well to her son that the scriptures were a treasure that he craved what she had. We must teach our children not simply that it is a commandment to serve, but also that obedience to the commandments brings blessings. They will see you living the gospel, but they need to know *why* you live the gospel.

You probably read your scriptures, for example, in part because it is a commandment. But reading scriptures is a commandment because it is such an ideal way for the Lord to bless us. Obedience entitles us to receive personal revelation that increases our understanding of the plan of salvation and also answers questions we might have about our own lives. These gifts from Heavenly Father are priceless, immediate repayments for our obedience, just as King Benjamin promised:

"And now, in the first place, he hath created you, and granted unto your lives, for which ye are indebted to him.

"And secondly, he doth require that ye should do as he hath commanded you; for which if ye do, he doth immediately bless you; and therefore he hath paid you. And ye are still indebted unto him, and are, and will be, forever and ever; therefore, of what have ye to boast?" (Mosiah 2:23–24).

As we fulfill our callings we are often reminded that heaven is close at hand. We receive personal inspiration regarding those within our stewardship and gain assurance that our Heavenly Father is mindful of each one of us. We watch lives change and see people we serve flourish in the gospel. Our children need to hear about these sacred experiences. Then they will know what is so wonderful about serving the Lord.

When you tell your children openly and unabashedly that you are experiencing blessings for your obedience, your children will crave such experiences of their very own. Service in the kingdom, and obedience to the commandments, is a very small price to pay to have the windows of heaven opened and understanding increased. Children who, in Monday night testimony meetings with their servant-parents, discover that such blessings are available will never begrudge the sacrifice living the gospel requires.

Elder Loren C. Dunn said, "Parents [should] bear their testimonies to their children in the home—actually express to your children exactly what it is about the Church you know to be true. If we think our children know these things just because they live in the same house with us, we are mistaken. We need to say the words so our families can feel the same spirit of testimony that we have felt. Family home evening is an ideal time for this to take place" ("How to Gain a Testimony," *Ensign*, January 1973, 85).

I had the enviable privilege of teaching my teenage sons' seminary classes for four years, and so I was able to bear testimony every day of the week. No matter how sleepy they were, they would have had to be snoring not to see how much I love the gospel and how deeply grateful I am to have it guide my life. Parents may cherish similar opportunities when they teach their children in Sunday School, priesthood, Young Women, or Primary. These are treasured opportunities for your children to hear your testimony and discover why you serve. If you don't hold callings that enable you to interact with your own children in a formal setting, you can embrace the opportunity at your weekly family home evening.

Any child who does not know what a tremendous comfort it can be to feel the Holy Ghost guide his or her life, does not fully appreciate the benefits of being a Latter-day Saint. The hours we expend fulfilling our callings are only part of the picture. Our children deserve to see the whole picture. When they do, they will bushwhack their way, sweat pouring down their faces, to obtain this pearl of great price.

CHAPTER 15

THE LEGACY YOU LEAVE

MIKAN TAYLOR WAS TWO YEARS OLD WHEN HER daddy was called to serve as a bishop. When she entered second grade her only memories of her dad were during his tenure as a bishop. On the first day of school, Mikan's teacher asked her to write her autobiography. She wrote: "My name is Mikan. There are six people in my family. I live with my mom. I have snakes for pets. My favorite subject is music. When I grow up I'd like to be a police officer."

Mikan's daddy, the bishop, came home late from a meeting one night and found Mikan's second-grade autobiography on the top of his domestic "in" basket.

"Did you read this?" he asked his wife in distress.

"I did," she replied with a sly smile.

"I can't believe she said that," the bishop lamented.

"I wouldn't worry about our daughter wanting to be a police officer," Mom teased. "At some time or other, *every* child wants to be a police officer."

"No, no," said Mikan's dad, becoming exasperated. "She wrote that she lives with her mom. It sounds like we're divorced or something."

Mom bit her lip to keep from saying what she was thinking. *Our daughter thinks you live at the church.*

But Dad sounded so forlorn, so wounded, that Mikan's mom was only too glad to bite her lip. She didn't even mind the faint taste of blood on the tip of her tongue.

Families make significant sacrifices so that valiant servants of the Lord can be about the Father's business. Doralee Madsen said that at one point her children actually thought their father's name was *Bishop* (in "How Do We Face Challenges as a Couple," *The Arms of His Love* [Salt Lake City: Deseret Book, 2000], 341). Parents may worry that these sacrifices will have an adverse effect on their children.

CONCERN FOR THE CHILDREN

It can tug at our heartstrings to witness the tears of our children as they make valiant attempts to connect with a parent who seems so elusive. They may run down the aisle and up onto the stand to sit on Dad's lap. They may cling to Mom's skirt as she climbs in the car. Older children may express their sorrow verbally at the absence of a parent. Or they may sulk or mourn when a parent can't come watch a ball game or take them to the zoo.

The parent remaining at home who witnesses a child's heartache may feel distress about her spouse's absence that she would never feel were it not for the child's pining. Sending the Lord's servant off to be about his work may not prove difficult, except for worry that it might have an adverse effect on the children. In addition, when conflict already exists in the mind of the supportive spouse, a child's pining may compound an existing personal struggle.

In the previous chapter we received reassurance that the pressure to set an example need not cause a child undue stress, nor does a parent's hard work necessarily disillusion a child. In this chapter we will see that a parent's frequent absence from home is not what harms the children of Church leaders.

How much easier it becomes to support the leader in your home when you are reassured that a parent's service will benefit, not harm, the children. You who support your spouses in demanding Church callings will want to be certain that your children are being blessed by a parent's Church service, not cheated.

FUTILE WORRIES

I remember feeling excited about my father's Church service when he served as a bishop. I didn't feel cheated or jealous of the Church, even though he was gone a lot. I thought it was an honor to have him serve. I watched the way others appreciated him. The youth greeted him, "Hey Bish . . ." as they extended a hand. When the telephone rang and people lined up outside the bishop's office, I knew that my dad had something valuable to offer all these people, and I respected him for his ability to help so many.

I believe that a parent's absence when about the Father's business does not traumatize a child in any way whatsoever. Children of busy Church servants can fare quite well even when one parent leaves home frequently in the service of the Lord.

Joseph F. Smith, the son of Church patriarch Hyrum Smith, became a prophet, even though his father left the family to serve missions, spent time in jail on false charges, and was ultimately martyred for his devotion to The Church of Jesus Christ of

Latter-day Saints. This child loved the cause his father loved, and embraced the cause his father embraced.

Virginia H. Pearce remembers feeling "a little deflated and sometimes irritated" when her mother was gone performing her duties as a Relief Society president. However, those feelings would "quickly evaporate" when Sister Pearce got a glimpse into the important work her mother was performing (in "The Power of Remembering," *The Arms of His Love,* 78).

Throughout the history of the Church, children have followed in the footsteps of devoted parents, developing the same conviction as the parents. The Church is strong and growing today because we have eighth-generation Latter-day Saints who are still following in their pioneer forefathers' footsteps.

Consider the dynamic parent-child teams in the Book of Mormon: Lehi and Nephi, Mosiah and Benjamin, Mormon and Moroni, Alma and his sons—these children of devoted parents were launched by their parents' example. They became valiant men in their own right, carrying on their parents' life work.

I have seldom felt so at-one with an individual as I have when reading the letters of my missionary son who bears fervent testimony of the very truths I have taught him throughout his life. I have been seen running across the house looking for my husband, waving my son's letter in the air, and shouting, "He gets it, honey, he really gets it!"

THE NATURE OF CHILDREN

The theatrics of young children may make us fear that they are suffering unbearably at their parent's absence. However, the children may simply be acting theatrical. Young children want a lot of things that, when they can't have them, may lead to a convincing show of distress.

The toddler may believe that if he expresses his emotions vehemently enough, perhaps he'll get what he wants. His drama might make us think that we are guilty of child abuse if we tell him no. However, a toddler's demonstrativeness may merely be an attempt to get his way, rather than an accurate barometer of his distress.

Children have been known to throw tantrums when they don't get their way, regardless of whether "their way" is good for them or not. As an adult, you will know whether a child is truly suffering from your spouse's absence. You can listen to the Spirit and determine if, indeed, it is appropriate to spend more time with a particular child. When you feel comfortable that the child is in perfectly good hands and perhaps just "wanting what he wants when he wants it," you can send your loved one off to serve the Lord without remorse or fear for the child's welfare. You need not let a child's immature developmental state color your commitment to serving the Lord wholeheartedly.

ABOUT AN ATTITUDE

A child's feelings about a parent's absence are not shaped by the amount of time the parent spends at home or away, but by how the children are taught to view the Church service. Children can learn that Church service is drudgery or they can learn that Church service is a privilege.

Surprisingly, the biggest influence on a child's attitude toward Church service is not how much time one parent does or does not spend away from home, but the *effect* of one parent's absence on the other parent. When Mom feels overburdened, and blames Dad's Church service, the children catch on, and they blame the Church too. The child develops a negative attitude, not because one parent is unavailable, but because his available parent appears upset.

"Nothing can take the place of the father in the home—but when the demands of job or calling keep the father away from the children for a time, their mother's attitude can make all the difference," said Orson Scott Card in a 1978 *Ensign* article ("How to Be a Full-Time Father," March 1978, 5).

The difference between a child who resents his parent's service and a child who embraces the cause for which his parent serves can be influenced by the attitude *both* parents exude regarding the service. If one of the parents feels resentful toward the cause, and the child senses a wedge between his folks, the child will resent the cause—not for taking one parent out of the home, but for the wedge that has grown between the parents. This is another reason it is so essential that you support your loved one in Church service. The testimonies of the children may be at stake.

A dynamic similar to the one we see when parents serve in the Church occurs in the families where the husband serves in the armed services. Our ward boundaries include a large Navy base, and 30 percent of the Melchizedek Priesthood holders in our ward are out to sea during the majority of their families' residencies in Jacksonville.

I notice a tremendous difference among the children of these sailors. Some couldn't be prouder to have their father serving this country. They want to grow up and serve their country just like their daddy. They wave a U.S. flag as the ships depart to sea, and they can't wait to tell Daddy what good girls or boys they have been when he returns.

Others' children curse the U.S. Navy. They complain because the Navy separates families for such long stretches of time. They count the days until their parent will be discharged, and they vow they will never enter the armed services themselves.

As I observe these various families, I am convinced that one of the major differences between the patriotic families who are proud of their military heritage and the resentful families that want out of the Navy is the attitude of the parent who remains home.

Attitudes become highly transparent in the parent's response to the question, "Where's Daddy?"

The response, "Honey, he's been asked to serve our country, and keep us free and safe from harm," communicates an entirely different message than, "He's at sea . . . *again*" (emphasis on the last syllable).

We can apply this principle to couples who support one another in Church service. The parent who remains home with the children while the other parent serves the Lord can indelibly affect the attitude of the children toward Church service.

The at-home parent who exudes excitement about a calling and respect for the leader's position will influence the children to feel excitement, respect, and even awe for their parent's leadership position. Children develop their own attitudes about a parent's demanding service by observing both their parents' attitudes toward the service.

Just as your attitude toward the gospel in general will rub off on your children, your attitude toward your spouse's Church service will rub off on the children. This provides you with a wonderful opportunity to teach correct principles. Your love for the gospel and your support for Church leaders will leave an indelible impression on your children, and they will desire to serve and support a Church servant with loyalty equal to yours.

Elder Jeffrey R. Holland said, "No child in this church should be left with uncertainty about his or her parents' devotion to the Lord Jesus Christ, the Restoration of His Church, and the reality of living prophets and apostles who, now as in earlier days, lead that Church according to the 'will of the Lord, . . . the mind of the Lord, . . . and the word of the Lord'" ("A Prayer for the Children," *Ensign,* May 2003, 85–86).

A child may suffer a little bit because one parent is often absent, but the child suffers doubly if the available parent is angry, resentful, or bitter about the absence. Then the child perceives the Church as hurting not only him (by taking away one parent) but the other parent as well (because he sees the available parent in pain), and a child will react far more adversely to a parent's pain than to his own.

The following ideas may help parents keep a cheerful attitude even when their partners can't be home as frequently as they would like.

Making Lemonade

Rumor has it that although Latter-day Saints eschew alcohol, we eat a lot of ice cream. I don't know if that is true of all LDS families, but our family is guilty as charged. We really like our ice cream. We don't eat the cheap ice cream either. We always buy brand names, with gooey chunks of candy inside. Traditionally, we eat ice cream on Sunday nights if the children have behaved well in church, and on Monday nights as a family home evening treat. Our family will eat pretty close to a half-gallon of ice cream each time we sit to enjoy the treat, so it's my job, as the mom, to always make sure our freezer is stocked with truly luscious ice cream.

One year I came home from a week-long trip to the Church Educational System conference in Provo, Utah, and all our ice cream had disappeared. I knew I had left the freezer well stocked, but in seven days the children had devoured six cartons of ice cream. I opened the freezer to serve ice cream on Sunday night as usual, but dig as I might, I couldn't find a single carton.

I looked to my husband, who had been in charge while I was gone: "Honey, where is the ice cream?"

He didn't look shocked. He didn't look angry. He didn't start scouting the room to discover who had a guilty face. He looked guilty himself! He averted my gaze and tried not to let me see his eyes. Finally, he spoke. "We ate ice cream every night while you were gone!" he admitted.

The kids hid their faces, as if to say it wasn't their fault. I looked around the room at my entire family, unitedly harboring this secret, and I burst into laughter. I laughed because they all looked so ridiculous. I laughed because they were so united in their guilt. And I laughed because they had eaten so much ice cream.

"It made it hurt less to have you gone," my husband revealed. "We were all kind of gloomy, so I thought the ice cream would cheer us up."

This technique, it turns out, is fairly common among families where one parent spends a lot of time away from home. In an effort to lighten their emotional load, family members who wait upon the busy parent choose to do something extra special for themselves.

They may not always choose ice cream as a way to treat themselves, but in one way or another, the supportive families find a way to divert their attention from pining for the missing family member. One extremely busy marketing manager travels for business and leaves his wife and two daughters more than he would like. While he is gone, Mrs. Rockwell and her two daughters pop popcorn, pop in a video, and climb into the large master bed together to cuddle up in the blankets and watch movies.

Other families treat themselves in such ways as the following:

- take time to watch home videos
- look through photo albums
- read bedtime stories a little longer than usual
- gather around the piano and choose favorite songs to sing
- play Pit, Uno, and other card or board games together
- play pool, Ping-Pong, or other table games together
- order their favorite take-out meals
- go out for their favorite fast food
- attend ball games together
- picnic together at the park

Does it sound like these families are celebrating in the absence of their loved one? They are! These families deliberately choose to celebrate together with those family members who are available rather than sit around and mourn the absence of the family member who is not available.

Consolation Prizes

Some might fear that indulging the children when one parent leaves will compromise the value of the absent parent. This is highly unlikely. Children don't generally value presents more than people. The love and attention of a parent outweighs any material possession or special outing. Unless the absent parent doesn't have much of a relationship with the children even when present, consolation prizes will remain just that—a consolation. The treats will never be as welcome as a parent's presence, but they will take away the sting of not having the parent home.

A consolation prize is not the same as a "brush-off" gift. There are parents who present a gift after an extended absence to excuse themselves from not spending time with the child. My hope is that Church leaders, on the other hand, return from an absence and reconnect with the child. They renew the relationship upon arrival and nurture that relationship during the hours they can spend together.

Consolation prizes do not compensate for a parent's absence. They just make it more bearable. When the parent returns, the renewal and a celebration of the parent-child relationship is healthy and warranted. Such celebrations occur when the parent and child join together in the same place at the same time to talk, laugh, play, whisper, tickle, share, and hug.

Even when your children grow up and leave home, you may desire a consolation prize for yourself if faced with the challenge of a frequently absent spouse. You might want to connect with dear friends you don't have time to see when your spouse is home. You can rent a video your spouse might consider boring, perhaps a foreign film or an "oldie." You can eat your favorite things for dinner—peanut butter sandwiches or carrots and dip. Of course you would eat a more balanced, healthy meal if your spouse were home, but this is a special occasion, being alone, so it's okay to indulge yourself and do something special. In addition, you can take advantage of the opportunity to render service, as discussed earlier in this book.

You generally have more time available when a spouse is absent. Husbands and wives typically spend a chunk of time together each day, sharing the day's experiences and unwinding together. When your spouse is not available for a traditional after-dinner conversation or "pillow talk" before bed, something or someone else can benefit from your own availability. The things you seldom find time to do during a typical workweek may squeeze their way into your schedule when your spouse is away serving in his or her Church calling. (One sister doesn't even mind her spouse's absences because she accomplishes so much while he is gone!)

Your tendency may be to fill those extra minutes with chores that you inherited because of your spouse's absence, but then your spouse's absence will become even more difficult than it was to begin with. When you use your extra time to catch up on chores, you may be doubly unhappy. You're unhappy because you miss your loved one, plus you're unhappy because your "to do" list just grew in size. Your goal should be to make your spouse's absence less painful, not more so.

Today's teenagers frequently use the phrase, "Get a life." From what I gather, this phrase means, "Make sure that you have activities and interests of your own that keep you excited, rather than depending on other people to give you a reason to live." If you consider this candid (albeit a bit irreverent) advice, you will immerse yourself in interesting activities regardless of whether or not your spouse is around. You can be supportive of your spouse, involving yourself in the work of the Lord, and still have your own agenda. You don't need to give up everything that is important to you to work beside your spouse, because there will be times when his responsibilities outpace yours. You don't want to find yourself pacing the floor and wringing your hands, waiting for an assignment. You can stay involved in some of the things that you have always been able to rely on to bring you joy.

The Potts family of Saylorsburg, Pennsylvania, has learned to celebrate in spite of one parent's absence. Becky and Rob parent four very active, lively boys. The boys love to run in the woods, turn over rocks, find critters, grind dirt into their fingernails, and act like, well—boys. Sister Potts likes to cross-stitch and read good books, and although extremely patient with her four rambunctious sons, she is glad they have a dad. Once Sister Potts traveled to the Church Educational System conference and rather than mourn her absence while she was gone, her family reveled in the things she doesn't particularly enjoy. Dad took the boys, their backpacks, and their sleeping bags, and they camped in the woods. They caught fish in a stream and slept under the stars. After a week they welcomed their mom back with open arms. But no one lost sleep at night because she was gone (unless it was from listening for bears!).

Survival Tools

Consider these light-hearted treats "survival tools" to be saved for difficult times. Consolation prizes, such as ice-cream sundaes, movies in the king-size bed, and camping under the stars are ways to relieve your emotional burdens. They take the "weight of the world" off your shoulders. They enable you to relax, laugh, and have fun. Treating yourself and your children in the midst of a trying time recharges your batteries so you can go on.

A TV/DVD player that we can plug into the AC/DC port in our car for children to watch when we travel long distances is a survival tool. We wouldn't normally let our children watch six movies in a single day, but when we are trying to keep them sane in close quarters, Walt Disney seems like a gift from heaven. Survival tools are gifts from heaven during precarious times in our lives. We can use them freely and be grateful for them. They will help us survive the requirements that are placed on families during a parent's period of demanding Church service.

People frequently ask me how as a therapist I can listen to people's problems all day long and still stay so happy. While I was in graduate school our professors taught us how to take on others' burdens without letting them bring us down. First and foremost, they taught us to take extraordinarily good care of ourselves. They taught us to fill our own buckets and nurture ourselves well. You will take on extra burdens when your loved one is serving the Lord. Therefore, you will want to take extraordinary care of yourself. Nurture yourself well. One way to treat yourself well is literally to treat yourself and/or your children to something delightful in your spouse's absence.

PROTECTING THE CHILDREN

The at-home parent may feel resentment at times because her load is so much heavier with an absent spouse. She may, indeed, think in her head, "Why?" "Is it worth it?" "Must the sacrifice be this great?" It may be tempting to let her own moments of discouragement or doubt seep into conversation with the children.

Should the temptation to complain to the children ever face you, do all in your power to resist the temptation. Pour your heart out on paper instead of on your children. Express your discouragement, doubts, or feelings of being unappreciated—whatever negative thoughts enter your mind—in an unfeeling, unimpressionable journal. Talk to a trusted priesthood leader and ask for a blessing that your burdens may be made light, as Alma's were. You might also fall upon your knees and beg Heavenly Father to bring peace to your own weary soul. In the Doctrine and Covenants we read: "If thou art sorrowful, call on the Lord thy God with supplication, that your souls may be joyful" (D&C 136:29).

When you arise from your knees you will be healed and can

face the children—who watch you so diligently—with a devoted and loyal demeanor. Your feelings of discouragement *will* go away. When they do you will marvel that you ever felt that way, and you will be infinitely grateful that you chose to protect your children from your pain. It would be a tragedy, once the feelings of discouragement left your heart, for them to remain in a child's.

Elder Jeffrey R. Holland has taught, "In matters of faith and belief, children are at risk of being swept downstream by this intellectual current or that cultural rapid. We as their parents must be more certain then ever to hold to anchored, unmistakable moorings clearly recognizable to those of our own household" ("A Prayer for the Children," 86).

A family's sacrifice is inevitable when they send a loved one off to serve the Lord. Elder M. Russell Ballard called them "sacred" sacrifices (*Ensign,* October 1998, 7). You can help your children cope with these sacrifices in the ways discussed in these last two chapters: clarifying their responsibilities, bearing firm and frequent testimony as to the joys of service, and verbalizing an unwaveringly supportive attitude.

Children As Companions

You can further help your children "buy into" the work in the same manner as you, the spouse of the Church servant, have done. You can work side by side with your children so your cause becomes their cause.

Many children gain a testimony of the truthfulness of the gospel serving alongside their parents. Fathers who can take their sons home teaching help their sons develop a testimony of home teaching. Mothers who invite their daughters to prepare and deliver a meal can help their daughters develop a testimony of service. These parents are serving anyway—and by inviting their children to serve alongside them, they can meet the needs of the members they serve, strengthen relationships with their own children, and help their children develop a testimony of the things they believe in (businessmen would call this "multitasking").

"I find that things I would have done by myself a few years ago I now do with one or two of my children. I still get everything done—but the children know I love them, that they will have a chance to be with me," said former bishop Robert Pixton (in Orson Scott Card, "How to Be a Full-Time Father," *Ensign*, March 1978, 5).

Orson Scott Card says, "I travel a lot to nearby towns—and some not so near. That time away from my family would be terrible, except that I usually take one of my children with me. When they get older, I even let them drive. In those hours together we rebuild anything that was lost while I was so busy during the intervening weeks" (ibid., 5).

My own father elected me to be his "home teaching companion" when he went to visit less-active families. I relished this special time to be together with my dad. He claimed it was his pinafored, blue-eyed toddler that got him in the doors of those homes where people otherwise might have turned him away.

PART FOUR

TAKING CARE OF THE FLOCK

CHAPTER 16

∞

INCREASING YOUR CAPACITY TO SERVE

A SIGN HANGS AT THE ENTRANCE TO THE GYM where my family works out. The sign reads: "To avoid injury, members must be familiar with proper use of equipment." My sons, who lift weights for football, work out regularly and know how to use the equipment pretty well. They continually add weight to their workout, and they are growing stronger and stronger. When I decided to start working out (not to grow stronger but to prevent osteoporosis), I asked my sons for help. When describing how to use the chest press, they warned me not to bring my arms back too far. "You'll hurt your shoulder if you do." Several months later, while working out, I overheard a personal trainer telling a guest the very same thing my sons had told me. "My roommate hurt his shoulder big-time by pulling back too far on this machine," the trainer said. "He can't even lift anymore."

These conversations reminded me that before I delve into weight lifting, I'd better know what I'm doing, or I'm going to get injured and it will set me back a long, long time. On the other hand, those who understand weight lifting grow stronger and stronger, increasing their capacity to lift more weight all the time.

This precise lesson applies to every one of us who wants to serve in the Lord's kingdom. As you serve beside your beloved mate, you too can grow stronger and stronger, continually increasing your capacity to serve. However, without understanding exactly what you're doing, it's possible to get injured and be set back for a long, long time.

Certain guidelines apply to weight lifting that can protect the lifter from injury: Have a personal trainer instruct you on the use of the machines. Don't lift more weight than you can safely handle. Watch your posture. Don't pull your arms too far back (on the chest press or the fly). Always use a spotter on the bench press.

Both Church leaders and their spouses will want to maintain their strength so they can continue to serve. As husbands and wives of Church servants, we are engaged in service right alongside our beloved spouses, and in addition, we are serving at home in high gear. We, of all people, will want to protect ourselves from injury.

Just as weight lifters grow stronger in their capacity to lift when they adhere to certain guidelines, servants of the Lord will increase their capacity to serve when they adhere to precautionary guidelines.

It is true that you can run only as fast as you have strength, and if you don't have enough strength, you simply can't do as much. However, you do have a lot to say about how much strength you gain and maintain.

The guidelines in this chapter briefly introduce some of the injuries Church servants can suffer and how to avoid the injuries.

The two chapters that follow reveal in detail ways to enlarge your service muscles.

INJURY RISKED: FEELING INADEQUATE

Guideline to Prevent Injury: Get Help

We've all felt inadequate at some time in our lives when asked to serve. When I was still in my twenties I was called to teach Gospel Doctrine in our ward. I was to team-teach with the stake patriarch, who was a spiritual giant and an unparalleled gospel scholar. We would trade off: he would teach one week and I would teach the next. I hesitated; no, I paused. Actually, I waited several minutes before I asked the bishop if he was sure he knew what he was doing. I could just imagine people arranging their schedules so they attended church the week he taught and stayed home the week I taught. I could see myself in the front of a vast chapel, chalkboard behind me, and not a soul in front.

I expressed my concerns to the bishop. I told him that I was not all that scholarly—particularly on the Old Testament, which was our course of study that year. Then he showed me the lesson manual. The Church had just eliminated the thick, chock-full-of-information resource and provided one page of questions for discussion. I would have even less scholarly material to draw upon than my predecessor! I was white with fear.

"Sister Smith," the bishop said, "there are a lot of gospel scholars in this ward who could teach this class. I called you because you *don't* know a lot." (Well, that sure made me feel better.) He continued, "We want our Gospel Doctrine teachers to teach by the Spirit and to rely less on scholarship. We know you are one who will teach by the Spirit."

He got that right. When I stood in front of the class, the only one up there who knew anything was the Holy Ghost. If I didn't rely on the Spirit I wouldn't have a thing to say.

When you feel overwhelmed about your ability to serve in a particular calling, you can always find comfort in the fact that you do not serve alone. We are each promised that when we are about the work of the Lord, we need not rely on our inadequate human abilities. If we seek the Lord, he will guide us.

"Go forth as I have commanded you; repent of all your sins; ask and ye shall receive; knock and it shall be opened onto you.

"Behold, I will go before you and be your rearward; and I will be in your midst, and you shall not be confounded" (D&C 49:26–27).

I find it so very amazing that the only qualification we need to serve in the kingdom of God is a willing heart. Whatever else we lack, the Lord can provide for us. He can provide us with time. He can provide strength, as he did for the captive people of Alma. He can provide knowledge. The Spirit teaches us things men cannot teach one another (see Gordon B. Hinckley, "The Father, Son, and Holy Ghost," *Ensign,* November 1986, 49). Whatever you need, the Lord will provide.

What then do you need to make you qualified to do his work? A desire to serve (see D&C 4:3).

And how do you know that you are not inadequate? How do you know if the job you have done is good enough? When you have served with all your heart, might, mind, and strength, you have done enough (see D&C 4:2). When you give all your heart, all your might, all your mind, and all your strength, you will stand blameless before God. He does not expect more than your all. So if you can't do everything, that means that everything was not expected of you. You are expected to do only what you can do. Your best is good enough.

It may seem at times as if you are being asked to give more than you have to give: more of your heart, might, mind, and strength than you possess. Such was the case with the widow of Zarephath who was asked to give Elijah the prophet her last measure of meal, such that she would not have enough for herself or her son (see 1 Kings 17). Should a prophet ever ask us to give more than we have to give, we can be assured that a miracle will occur in our lives, just like it did for the widow of Zarephath. When you feel as if you have no more energy, no more time, no more ideas, you can be assured that if you are asked to perform a task, your barrels will miraculously be filled with energy, time, ideas, or whatever it is you lack.

The law of tithing is an ideal example of this principle. We are not commanded to give more than we have. We are commanded to give a portion of what we have. We can be assured that if the Lord asks 10 percent we will be able to afford 10 percent, even if it takes a miracle to fill our barrels with meal.

INJURY RISKED: BECOMING OVERWHELMED AND OVERBURDENED

Guideline to Prevent Injury: Sensible Boundaries

Personal boundaries are much like invisible shields or bubbles that surround us. We get to decide what comfortably can enter that shield, and what we feel more comfortable leaving out of the shield. We all have personal space, and we can become uncomfortable and feel violated if someone stands too close to us or puts his or her face too close to ours. Likewise, we all have emotional boundaries, and if others cross them, we will feel claustrophobic, as if we are being robbed of the freedom to make decisions within our own "bubbles." It would be a boundary invasion, for example, if you told a friend you wanted to go to sleep at 10:00 at night, and that friend repeatedly called you on the telephone at 10:15 or 10:30 or 11:00 at night.

We all need to set personal boundaries in order to function at our optimal ability. We need to sleep a certain number of hours at night. We need a certain number of hours at home to keep up a house. We need some private time to ponder and pray. If others don't respect our personal boundaries, we may be deprived of the time we need to function optimally.

To understand the concept of boundaries, imagine the Savior preaching to a crowd of people that pressed in on him so closely he could not be seen by the majority of his audience. To avoid being thronged by the crowd, the Savior created some personal space. He sat in a boat a little way out from the land, and the multitude was forced to stay on the shore. "And it came to pass, that, as the people pressed upon him to hear the word of God, he . . . saw two ships standing by the lake. . . . And he entered into one of the ships, which was Simon's, and prayed him that he would thrust out a little from the land. And he sat down, and taught the people out of the ship" (Luke 5:1–3).

The Savior loved the people he taught, and he rejoiced that they wanted to be near him, but if some huddled too close, all couldn't hear, so he needed to establish some boundaries.

Have you ever had a little child try to hug you? They are not tall enough to hug you around the shoulders, so they end up hugging you around the knees, and although you love them, and it's great that they love you, when they hug you around the knees it prevents you from walking and may even cause you to topple over! Sometimes little children want to climb in your lap and stay there for hours and hours and hours. Although you love them and it's great that they love you, you have to set a boundary so you can function.

Sometimes those we serve are so excited about the fact that we love them and are willing to give of ourselves that they want to crowd our space and "sit on our laps" all day long.

You've undoubtedly read the story in which Jesus cast a legion of devils out of a man and allowed the devils to enter a herd of swine, which subsequently ran into the sea and drowned. After the devils depart, the man who has been healed wants to join the Savior and travel with him: "Now the man out of whom the devils were departed besought him that he might be with him: but Jesus sent him away, saying, Return to thine own house, and shew how great things God hath done unto thee. And he went his way, and published throughout the whole city how great things Jesus had done unto him" (Luke 8:38–39). Even though the man wanted to stay with Jesus, the Savior refused to allow the man to stay with him.

This decision may have been in the best interest of the healed man, who needed to learn to live a normal life. Or it may have been a decision in the best interest of the giver, who needed to focus on his ministry, without the healed man among his companions. In either case, notice that it was the giver's decision to determine the limits of the gift, not the receiver's. It is the giver's job to set boundaries, not the receiver's.

DETERMINING THE TERMS OF THE GIFT

Becoming overwhelmed is inevitable when we allow others to invade our personal boundaries, when we give beyond what we can comfortably give. If you can't afford the time, or the money, or the physical exertion, the act of service will drain you and cause undue concern. Therefore, if you want to avoid becoming overburdened, you are the one who must determine that you can afford (financially, emotionally, physically) to render the service for which you volunteer.

You can't expect the people whom you serve to know how much you can or cannot give. You know the breadth and depth of all your responsibilities, and you know your own capacity to give better than the person to whom you are giving. The giver is the only one who knows all the demands on his time, as well as his capacity to give, and is therefore entirely responsible for setting clear boundaries.

The giver has the right, even the responsibility, to determine the amount of service he wants to render, the length of service, the frequency of the service, and the nature of the service. We might not know why a giver gives in a certain way, but it is the prerogative of the giver to set the terms of his service, not the prerogative of the taker.

President Harold B. Lee lived in the ward where I grew up, yet it was very rare for him to attend our ward. One special fast Sunday he attended fast and testimony meeting all by himself, without any security people. He actually stood from the front row of the overflow seats and bore his testimony; it was the last testimony of the day. I was thrilled. I ached to meet him and shake his hand, and I kept looking at him out of the corner of my eye while the meeting closed. Immediately following the closing prayer I darted to the back of the chapel, where he had stood, and tried to catch him. However, as I was headed to the back of the chapel, he was headed for the back door. I walked as fast as I could to catch up with him, but he walked still faster. I remained all alone in the hall as he left the building.

At the time, I was disappointed that the prophet chose to depart so soon after the meeting, and not linger to greet people or slow down when he heard the patter of footsteps following him. But now I realize that prophets need to rest too. He chose to give us a very generous gift that day—his testimony. He chose not to linger and shake hands. I have learned to thoroughly respect his choice to give what he felt he was in a position to give, without regretting that he did not give more.

As givers, we all will want to consider our own capacity to give when rendering service, as well as the needs of the recipient. Do you recall how upset Mary and Martha were when Jesus did not return to Bethany as soon as they sent word that Lazarus was ill? (see John 11:21, 32). Only Christ knew his reasons for the delay. Mary and Martha didn't. It was not appropriate for the receivers of the service to dictate the conditions of the service. The greatest giver of all determined the nature of the gift he would give—and look how much more glorious a gift he gave than the one Mary and Martha asked for!

A bishop may not immediately write a welfare check in the full amount that is requested as soon as it is requested. The bishop knows his capacity to give, whereas the recipient of the money does not. In addition, the bishop may have a gift to give that is even more valuable than the check. Keeping the needs of the recipient in mind, the bishop may teach the recipient to set up a budget or help the recipient obtain better employment. The recipient of the gift may not understand the limits of the gift, but it is still the privilege of the giver to set the terms of the gift.

Ideally, the gift will be a "win-win" gift—a win for the giver and a win for the receiver. However, this can occur only if the giver chooses the limits of the gift, so he doesn't feel he is giving more than he is capable of giving. Only when we give gifts that are within our capacity to comfortably give can we avoid becoming overburdened.

If someone with authority asks us to give a gift beyond our seeming capabilities, the Lord will strengthen our backs and enable us to fulfill assignments that may at first seem daunting to us.

INJURY RISKED: RESENTMENT

Guideline to Prevent Injury: Honor Your Priorities

Have you ever rearranged your entire day's schedule so you could bake a casserole for somebody who was ill, and when you dropped it off, her refrigerator was so full you couldn't even find a place for your pan? Have you ever given up your favorite Saturday morning activity so you could participate in the ward work party, and when you arrived there were so many people there you couldn't find a leaf to rake? Have you ever diligently prepared a lesson and none of the students in the class showed up for you to present it?

Such experiences can be avoided, so resentment does not occur.

Resentment can occur if you give up something that is an extremely high priority to you in order to do something of low priority. For example, if your son is the starting quarterback in a championship football game, and you miss his game in order to scoop mulch, you're going to be extremely disappointed to discover a dozen mulch scoopers with shovels in hand. If your son's game was a high priority, you'll feel comfortable missing it only for something of higher priority. Were you to show up and find your services desperately needed, you wouldn't regret missing your son's game. Conversely, if your calendar was empty on Saturday morning, and you didn't have anything of high priority to do, you'd enjoy sitting around and chatting with other dedicated Saints, even if the mulch scooping wasn't a super-high priority. At least it was higher than what you would have done instead.

You can protect yourself from giving up something of high priority to do something of low priority if you do your homework. There are ways to discover how high a priority the service project is compared to what you are giving up in order to render service. It's possible to make sure the person truly needs the type of service you intend to render.

At our local high school, parents are required to work in the concession stand during the football games, but there are usually so many parents there we can barely reach the sodas. When my turn to work in the concession stand arrived, I called to see how many parents were scheduled. There were plenty, so instead of scrapping for nachos and hot dog buns, I volunteered to help my husband keep stats. Sure, it wasn't as social an environment as the concession stand, but the service was truly needed, whereas another body grilling hot dogs wasn't.

This guideline for avoiding resentment considers both what the servants *give up* and also what they *give*. Make sure what you give is as high a priority to the recipient as what you give up in order to render the service.

Consider one more crucial technique for avoiding resentment.

The first year of our marriage Bret and I decided we wanted to render service at Christmastime. We called a local charity to obtain the name of a needy family that might not have any gifts for Christmas without our help. We obtained the name of a mother, a father, and two children who lived in a trailer park not far from the university we attended. Although we were poor students ourselves, we enjoyed shopping for this needy family, wrapping gifts, and baking. A few weeks before Christmas we arrived at their doorstep with a tree, a bag of gifts, and a basket of food. For a few moments we thought we had stopped at the wrong door. Through the window we saw a tree donned with lights and ornaments; a television with a VCR flashed in the background (those were the days when VCRs were expensive, and we certainly didn't own one!). The couple opened the door, and we saw a plethora of gifts already under their tree. We were actually embarrassed by our contribution; it paled so in comparison to what they already had. We mumbled our apologies. We thought they might be offended by our treating them as though they were needy when clearly they were not. They weren't embarrassed in the least. "Oh, we gave our name to a bunch of different agencies," they explained. "They all provided Christmas for us."

We could have avoided this situation if we had known somehow which families were truly needy, and had been able to select a truly needy family. However, we were too young and naïve to know to ask. When it's not possible to do some homework and determine the priority of the service you are about to render, you can use another technique for avoiding resentment.

Notice that my husband and I were perfectly happy with our decision to serve until we discovered the service wasn't needed. As Santa's elves, we had a great time selecting a tree and we laughed until we cried when trying to tie it on top of our little Toyota Corolla. We giggled together as I tried to show Bret how to tie a quilt, and he kept poking his finger with a quilting needle. We raced wind-up toys down the aisle at K-Mart before we bought them. The process of serving was thoroughly enjoyable to us.

It really didn't matter whether or not the people appreciated our service. What mattered is that we found joy in the act of service. If we had dropped our donation off at the county health department and had them deliver it to the "needy" family directly, we would have never known the response, and we could have remained delighted with our opportunity to serve.

You can't control how someone will respond to your acts of service, but you can do something about your attitude toward the service. When choosing to serve, you can avoid resentment if you focus on the process of service itself, regardless of the end result of the service.

When I read about the Savior offering service, I can tell that he loved what he was doing. There is no place he would rather be than blessing the lives of his children on this earth. One of the most beautiful examples of his attitude toward service can be found in the synoptic gospels. Mark chapter 10 reads:

"And they brought young children to him, that he should touch them: and his disciples rebuked those that brought them.

"But when Jesus saw it, he was much displeased, and said unto them, Suffer the little children to come unto me, and forbid them not: for of such is the kingdom of God. . . .

"And he took them up in his arms, put his hands upon them, and blessed them" (vv. 13–14, 16).

It appears that the Savior *wanted* to perform this act of service. Not only was he teaching his disciples a very important principle about the nature of children and the nature of heaven, he relished the processes of blessing the children.

I get this same feeling when I read of the Savior's visit to the Nephites. He had been with these people for some time and it was time for him to go. He had work to do elsewhere. But when he looked into their eyes to say good-bye and saw their love and their sorrow at his pending departure, he could hardly bear to leave them. He wanted to stay. He wanted to bless them. He enjoyed serving them and delighted in the moments he spent in their midst. Chapter 17 of 3 Nephi paints the ultimate picture of tender love and caring. I cannot even fathom a scene more glorious. I cannot even fathom what could not be written.

INJURY RISKED: BURNOUT

Guideline to Prevent Injury: Don't Spin Your Wheels

Many years ago a bishop asked me to baby-sit two small boys a couple of evenings a week while their mother attended real estate classes. I was happy to do this act of service because I saw that this sister truly needed help. However, the mother attended the real estate course only a couple of times, and before a month went by, she stopped attending. Not knowing she had stopped attending class, I continued to come over and watch her boys.

I had given quite a bit, and it was all I could do endure to the three-month mark. When I discovered it had all been for naught and that this woman had not done a thing to change, I felt even more exhausted. The bishop who asked me to serve comforted me with this assurance: "We have to give everybody an opportunity to change, but we can't do the changing for them. Your service wasn't for naught because you gave the mother an opportunity she would have not had without you."

Nothing is more exhausting in Church service than the feeling that you are doing all the work and the person you are serving isn't putting forth any effort of his own. When you put forth all the effort you may feel you are spinning your wheels. Think about the expression "spinning your wheels." Can you imagine trying to push a cart whose wheels just sink deeper and deeper into the mud? You push harder and harder, and the wheels just go around and around in the very same spot. Such a challenge will exhaust even the most enthusiastic Saint.

You can avoid spinning your wheels when expending energy in service if you look for some small signs that those you serve are putting forth a little bit of effort of their own.

Even humorists know you can't change someone who doesn't want to change. The quintessential therapist joke asks, "How many therapists does it take to change a light bulb?" The answer: "It depends on whether the light bulb wants to change." So it is with those we serve. We can't help someone who does not want our help.

It's difficult to know when you are putting forth all the effort, and the recipient of your service has no intention of changing. How much effort do you expend on someone before you decide you are working harder to effect change than the recipient of your service? President Joseph L. Bishop, who was the president of the Missionary Training Center in Provo, Utah, for many years, was also the mission president in the Argentina Buenos Aires North Mission when my husband served as a missionary there. President Bishop taught the missionaries to teach only the families who were progressing. A family was progressing if they were reading their scriptures, praying, and attending church. When a family stopped progressing, President Bishop suggested that the missionaries move on and teach someone else. In 1979 the Argentina Buenos Aires North Mission was baptizing more than 200 people a month. There were plenty of people who wanted to hear the gospel. It did not make sense to deprive the honest in heart of the opportunity to hear the truth because the missionaries were too busy teaching someone who wasn't serious about changing his life.

This does not mean that investigators have to read their scriptures 365 days a year and attend church fifty-two weeks in a row. It means they needed to be making *some* effort of their own.

How long do we continue to work with individuals who make no effort on their own? How many times do we drop by someone's home to have the lights flicked off and our knocks ignored? The Holy Ghost will prompt us to know the occasions when we should continue our efforts, even though progress does not seem imminent.

FINDING A MATCH

I've discovered that the safest guideline to follow when deciding how much effort to expend on a person with a tenuous interest in change is to match my effort to theirs. When your efforts to fellowship are commensurate with the individual's efforts to change, you won't feel like you are doing all the work, spinning a wheel that won't budge out of its rut.

Consider the process of making friends with a new neighbor. You might invite the neighbor over for root beer floats one night to assess whether or not they are interested in a friendship with you. Then you wait to see if they invite you over to swim in their pool. If they do, it shows they have an interest in the relationship, and you will reciprocate their kindness. However, if you invite them over for root beer floats one week, and to a cookout the next, and for family home evening the next, to a professional baseball game the next, and out on the jet skis the next, and they either turn down your invitations or refrain from reciprocating, it becomes obvious that they are not interested in the friendship. You are the only one putting forth any effort.

You don't need to see evidence of an Alma the Younger conversion experience in the people you fellowship—just clues that these individuals are receptive to your efforts. Receptivity might come in the form of returning telephone calls or allowing you to drop by for a short visit. By waiting to see if people are receptive, you won't be making sacrifices that go unappreciated. You may call them on the telephone or offer a ride to a meeting, but you won't embarrass them by expending all kinds of effort that is not acknowledged, welcomed, or reciprocated. Your efforts will be at a level they are comfortable with. Your efforts will be appropriate for the level of commitment these individuals are willing to expend at the moment.

A bishop made it a practice to telephone every less-active

member in his ward at least once a month just to see how they were doing. He left a message on the answering machine if the people weren't home. If they returned the call, he asked how they were doing and if he could be of service in any way. Months and months went by, and hundreds of telephone calls were made. Eventually some of the individuals started returning the bishop's calls. The individuals who returned his calls were then asked if they would allow him to drop by and visit. Those individuals who allowed a personal visit were invited to attend Sunday meetings. Those who attended Sunday meetings sometimes asked to meet with the bishop in his office. Gradually, with a little effort on the part of the bishop, and a little effort on the part of the less-active members, numerous people came back into activity. Eventually the bishop had the privilege of traveling to the temple with some of them to be present when they took out their endowments. Taking a day off work to travel to the temple is a pretty involved act of service on the part of a bishop. However, when the members are making a pretty involved effort to change, the extent of the service feels right to both of them.

I have found that I never feel I am needlessly spinning my wheels when I match the pace of my service with the pace of the people I serve. I try to focus on those who are putting forth *some* effort. It doesn't matter how much effort, as long as they are putting forth some. Sometimes I feel as if I am traveling like a snail down the road, but at least I am moving! And that's a lot more fulfilling than staying in the same place and digging a deeper and deeper rut.

INJURY RISKED: DISCOURAGEMENT

Guideline to Prevent Injury: Focus on the Principle of Obedience

One of the hardest things for celestial-kingdom-bound Latter-day Saints to accept is that not everybody on planet Earth has the same ambitions we have. We gasp to learn that there are people who know the Book of Mormon is the word of God but who don't even try to abide by its teachings. It is entirely unfathomable to us that someone could say they know the Church is true but choose not to join. Nevertheless, amongst the many different individuals it takes to make up a world live a population of people that are entirely content with the world's ways. They have no desire to change whatsoever, even at a snail's pace.

The principle we must remember is that we labor not necessarily because we are guaranteed results. We labor because we are commanded to labor. And one of the reasons we are commanded to labor is because it helps perfect us.

In Moroni chapter nine we read about a people who refuse to repent.

"And now behold, my son, I fear lest the Lamanites shall destroy this people; for they do not repent, and Satan stirreth them up continually to anger one with another.

"Behold, I am laboring with them continually; and when I speak the word of God with sharpness they tremble and anger against me; and when I use no sharpness they harden their hearts against it; wherefore, I fear lest the Spirit of the Lord hath ceased striving with them.

"For so exceedingly do they anger that it seemeth me that they have no fear of death; and they have lost their love, one towards another; and they thirst after blood and revenge continually" (vv. 3–5).

It would really be discouraging to work with such a wicked people. It would be very easy to throw up your arms and give up. Like another prophet, Jonah, you might want to get as far away from such a people as possible.

Notice Mormon's response to the Lamanites' wickedness in verse 6:

"And now, my beloved son, notwithstanding their hardness, let us labor diligently; for if we should cease to labor, we should be brought under condemnation; for we have a labor to perform whilst in this tabernacle of clay, that we may conquer the enemy of all righteousness, and rest our souls in the kingdom of God."

Moroni serves because it's a commandment. He doesn't hold out much hope for these people but he maintains plenty of hope for himself. He knows he will be brought under condemnation unless he continues to minister despite its seeming uselessness. He also knows that by continuing to minister, he personally will conquer the enemy of all righteousness. His ministering will bring about his own salvation, if not that of those to whom he ministers.

This point was brought home to me in a lighter, even humorous manner. Our ward consists of a lot of beach dwellers. The ward boundaries include a narrow strip of land, bordered on the east by the Atlantic Ocean and on the west by the Intracoastal Waterway. People who live in the ward boundaries call themselves "islanders." Due to the geographic location of the ward, a large number of homeless people live within the ward boundaries. Living at the beach is convenient for the homeless because the climate is temperate: less cold in the winter and less hot in the summer. The homeless can bathe at the beach, and they can camp in the woods. The churches on the "island" are frequently accosted by the homeless for various handouts. (Once a homeless man found his way into an LDS ward building and spent the night. The early-morning seminary teacher almost had a heart attack when she arrived to teach the next morning!)

One of the homeless came to our building one Wednesday night and told the bishop he needed money to buy disposable diapers for his baby. The bishop asked the new father to wait at the building for a few minutes. Then the bishop drove to the grocery store on the corner and bought a big bag of Huggies. He returned with seventeen dollars' worth of diapers and gave them to the man. An hour or so later the bishop was again shopping at the grocery store. Whom should he see at the customer service counter trying to return the Huggies? Yep. The pretend father. The homeless man recognized the bishop and offered a sly smile. The bishop laughed out loud, went over, and put his arm around the bony shoulders, and squeezed. "You had me there, brother. The diapers thing—that was good." Affection was exchanged between these two men; it took only a smile, but it was enough to tell this homeless man that no one was condemning him for his duplicity. The bishop was okay with the fact that some people choose not to launch themselves when blessed with a little momentum. At least the bishop was doing his part in giving the homeless man opportunity.

We may think our efforts have been wasted when we expend considerable effort ministering to someone who refuses to change. We might not be able to muster the good humor the bishop mustered when he discovered his gift being returned. However, efforts to bless mankind are never wasted.

We clothe the naked, feed the poor, visit the sick and afflicted because we are obedient. They may not change, but we will. We will become sanctified as we serve.

Because the Lord directs this work, you and your loved one will experience miracles throughout your service. You may not see every soul you serve respond, but you will still witness miracles as individuals do embrace the truth, accept the gospel and the blessings it provides, repent of their sins, and come unto Christ.

We must protect ourselves from negative emotions that may

thwart our desire to participate in the work. How sad it would be to work and work in a mine digging for gold and to quit just before you struck the mother lode. Don't give in to discouragement or resentment. There is too much joy in being an active participant in the work of the Lord during the times that miracles do occur and lives do change.

CHAPTER 17

⌒

ULTERIOR MOTIVES

WITH A SPOUSE IN A LEADERSHIP POSITION, YOU will likely become involved in a whole lot of service. You will serve side by side with your eternal companion in the Church and you will serve more than ever in your home. In addition, you are also likely to find ways to serve the Lord on your own and thus further this great work.

Despite its constancy, none of this service has to become burdensome. You need never experience negative emotions such as burnout, frustration, or resentment. The final secret to serving alongside your spouse with joy and enthusiasm lies in serving with pure motives. Whether you are serving in your own calling, rendering service at home so a spouse can fulfill his or her calling, or offering service that is not related to a specific calling, service retains its luster only when you aim to serve out of selfless motives. If your motives become contaminated, you may come to resent the service you render.

Just as people may lift weights for ulterior motives (to flaunt a skimpy swimsuit at the beach rather than to stay healthy), some folks may—without realizing it—serve their fellowman for ulterior or selfish motives.

GOSPEL INSIGHTS

In a 1984 address, Elder Dallin H. Oaks enumerated a hierarchy of motives for service. Elder Oaks presents his motives in "ascending order from the lesser reasons to the greatest." His list progresses thus:

1. hope for earthly reward
2. desire for companionship
3. fear of punishment
4. sense of duty
5. hope of eternal reward
6. charity—the pure love of Christ

Notice that only the highest motive, the pure love of Christ, focuses on the recipient of the service. All the other motives are for the benefit of the giver. The servant serves not to bless the lives of the needy, but to bless his own life.

"Since we are imperfect beings, most of us probably serve for a combination of reasons," Elder Oaks said, "and the combinations may be different from time to time as we grow spiritually. But we should all strive to serve for the reasons that are highest and best" ("Why Do We Serve?" *Ensign,* November 1984, 13).

Lesser motives are not evil. How can service to one's fellowman be bad? However, Elder Oaks said lesser motives are "not worthy of Saints." And lesser motives may bring us worldly pleasure, instead of heavenly treasure.

How can you determine if you possess these lesser motives that are not worthy of Saints? First, you can ask yourself, "What is my primary reason for performing this act of service?" The most obvious answer is, "Because the person is suffering." However, if you delve a little deeper into your mind you might discover answers such as these:

> "I'd feel guilty if I didn't help."
> "All the other elders in the quorum will be there."
> "I need the service hours."
> "I need the CBPs (Celestial Brownie Points)."
> "The bishop will be so proud of me."

Some may serve because it's required by the university they attend, or it may help them win a college scholarship. Some serve because it looks good on a resume. Some serve because their child sees more playing time in the ball game with a parent-coach. All of these motives focus primarily on the giver and only incidentally on the receiver.

Some people don't even recognize that they possess ulterior motives until they stop and ponder their motives, and realize they are really serving to alleviate guilt, to engender gratitude, or to assure eternal rewards.

Please remember, once again, it's not wicked to serve with a lesser motive. It's just not as satisfying. Because you are trying to make supporting a spouse in his or her Church service a delight, not a drag, it's essential that you not "white-knuckle" your service. You don't need to grit your teeth, "muster the stamina," and "do your duty." As a willing and able servant of the Lord, you can learn to tap a motive that turns the opportunity to serve into a joyous privilege.

A SECOND OPINION

In the 1950s American psychologist Lawrence Kohlberg developed a theory of "moral development," wherein he postulated certain motives for human behavior. A simplification of his theory illuminates five motives that help explain why humans make particular choices:

1. fear of punishment
2. hope of reward
3. desire to conform
4. sense of duty
5. awareness of others' needs

Kohlberg believed we experience each of these motives in stages. We go through a developmental process, first serving at a less mature level of development, and as we mature we serve at higher levels of development. Initially we all make choices because we fear punishment. As we grow older and more mature, we then make our choices out of hope for a reward. As we grow more mature still, we make decisions out of a desire to conform, then out of a sense of duty, and finally because of an awareness of others' needs.

These motives sound a lot like those Elder Oaks enumerated. Kohlberg believed, however, that few people ever really reach the last stage of moral development, awareness of others' needs. He felt it was beyond the developmental process of most humans to do things for purely altruistic reasons.

Elder Oaks, on the other hand, *expects* us to serve for altruistic reasons. The entire purpose for addressing the subject was to help Saints develop charity, or the pure love of Christ.

I agree with Kohlberg's observation that motives are hierarchical and that we serve with more altruistic motives as we mature. Obtaining charity is a process and we may spend a lot of years serving with lesser motives on our way to developing the pure love of Christ.

Fear of Punishment

Most of us, by the time we reach adulthood, will have grown beyond the fear of punishment. The bishop doesn't ground those who refuse to go home teaching, after all. So although fear of punishment doesn't motivate many adults, the hope of reward can certainly get us moving in the morning.

Hope of Reward

It may not appear that members of The Church of Jesus Christ of Latter-day Saints serve for rewards because there is no paid ministry in our church. Neither does service in the Church guarantee scholarships or employment opportunities. It doesn't bring money or rank advancement. We don't even get a crystal bowl with "twenty years of service" engraved on the side when we reach such milestones.

Members of the Church may appear entirely altruistic, serving with no hope for reward. Thus we might assume that Church members' motives are as pure as spring water, uncontaminated by selfish desires.

You're laughing because those "in the know" know this is not the case. Members of The Church of Jesus Christ of Latter-day Saints serve with all sorts of motives, just like the rest of the world. Our motives, however, are less tangible, less obvious. We may not be consciously aware that we are seeking personal rewards, because the rewards we receive from serving are largely intangible.

One of the most popular rewards for service is the recognition of men. I'm not talking about "Hollywood hunks" kind of men—I mean mankind, both men and women, who observe us serving and whisper, "Wow!"

We enjoy the attaboys, the oohs and aahs, our fellow Saints

shower upon us. We enjoy the reputation we develop as compe-
tent and capable and "the person you can always count on." We
may even swell with pride when someone we have served stands at
the pulpit on fast Sunday and sings our praises. We look forward
to compliments such as "You really outdid yourself."

Legend tells of a teacher who, long ago, was teaching a
Gospel Doctrine class about the Mormon pioneers, and with the
best of intentions she wanted her students to gain an appreciation
for the shape and size of the Salt Lake Tabernacle. So she hung
streamers in the chapel, starting in the center and extending them
around the entire room like a giant Ferris wheel (a definite case
of asking for forgiveness rather than permission). Now, this
teacher may have truly wanted her students to develop a huge
admiration for the pioneers. Instead, they developed a huge admiration for her. They talked for decades, not about the extravagance of the Tabernacle, but about the extravagance of the
teacher.

Sometimes we serve without even recognizing that we hope
for a reward. We may think we are serving with pure motives, and
it is not until something goes awry that we discover our motives
were contaminated by a hope of a reward.

A darling young couple I once knew found themselves child-
less after several years of marriage. At the same time, in the ward
lived a single mother of a teenage boy. The mother was mentally
ill, and the teenage boy was giving her all kinds of trouble. This
couple took the teenage boy under their wings and treated him
like their own son. The husband played sports with the boy. The
wife fixed up a room in their house for him, and he lived with the
couple for months at a time, particularly when the mother wasn't
functioning optimally. Everybody seemed to benefit from the
arrangement, until eventually the couple asked the boy's mother if

they could adopt the teenager so he could truly be their own son. Even though the mother was handicapped, there was still a pretty solid bond between mother and son, and they both turned down this couple's offer. As a result, the couple grew more and more distant from this young man, and the young man was in danger of losing the role models he had treasured.

In this story, it seems the couple's own need for children began to overshadow their desire to bless the young man's life. With pure motives the relationship could have continued indefinitely on a positive note. Throughout the Church, mentoring relationships do bring lasting satisfaction to both adults and children. We see it happen in the Scouting program and in the Young Women and Young Men programs and in seminary. These relationships prove successful when the giver keeps the needs of the recipient in mind, rather than focusing on his or her own needs.

Desire to Conform

What Kohlberg labeled "the desire to conform" Elder Oaks labeled the "desire to obtain good companionship." This lesser motive might also appear unlikely for members of the Church. As Latter-day Saints, we don't necessarily get to choose our companions when we serve. We are assigned ward boundaries, assigned home teaching companions, assigned home teaching families, and assigned to a particular calling. We may or may not desire the companionship of the people we are asked to serve. That is not supposed to matter. The Church is designed so we won't be corrupted by ulterior motives, and we do not choose congregations or committees based on how many rich and famous people fill the pews.

Outside the Church, where you can usually choose whatever congregation you want to attend, and you can choose which committees you want to volunteer to serve on, the motive of serving to obtain good companionship flourishes. I often observe this motive—serving to obtain good companionship—among those not of our faith. Many of my clients serve busily in the churches they attend. In the South, the Christian churches often sponsor a Vacation Bible School (VBS) during the summer months. For a week the children attend a summer camp where they learn about God. VBS is run entirely by volunteers, and they put on quite an elaborate program. Frequently the teachers dress up in costumes. They may make piñatas that hang from the ceiling or huge props to place on the floor. VBS is a lot of work and a lot of fun for the volunteers. However, my clients readily admit their sole reason for volunteering is that they like "hanging out" with the other moms who participate. Kind of like Kiwanis Club or Rotary Club, to them their church is a service club where they can socialize as they serve.

Even though our church is designed otherwise, Latter-day Saints may be motivated by the desire to obtain good companionship as well. Such Saints will "ward shop," or request a certain visiting teaching route, or only accept callings to serve when they like the people they would be serving with.

None of these other motives is necessarily bad. You certainly can't call rendering service a sin of commission, even if the primary motive is to obtain good companionship. Lots of people are blessed by these socialite servers. However, Elder Oaks called this motive "unworthy of Saints" ("Why Do We Serve?" 14). Such a motive can backfire and rob the server of the true joy that comes from serving out of pure motives.

A Sense of Duty

These "lesser" motives are listed in hierarchical order, from least to greatest, so the more mature you become, according to

Kohlberg, the more mature your motives. Therefore, by the time someone reaches the point where he is serving out of a sense of duty, he is a fairly mature human being. He has overcome some of his fears and his selfish desires. He no longer serves to obtain the praise of men, or to obtain good companionship. Serving out of duty is a highly praiseworthy reason to serve.

The hymn "Because I Have Been Given Much" (*Hymns* [Salt Lake City: The Church of Jesus Christ of Latter-day Saints, 1985], no. 219) teaches us just that; we, who have been given abundant blessings, must give back. King Benjamin tells us that we serve because we are indebted to the Lord (see Mosiah 2:17–24). I have heard missionaries claim that they served the Lord for two years because "it's the least I could do after all he has given me."

I imagine many, many Latter-day Saints serve out of a sense of duty, and there is nothing wrong with that. In fact, Kohlberg believed that few human beings ever serve for a greater reason. Not many of us ever get beyond this point. The most noteworthy motive most men ever attain is to serve because of a sense of duty.

As members of the Church, however, we learn that it is possible to serve with even higher motives. The hope of an eternal reward, and the awareness of others' needs, or charity, are in a different category than the other motives.

THE ARM OF FLESH

You may wonder what's so bad about serving with these lesser motives. Why not serve out of fear of punishment, desire for good company, or hope of reward? The recipients of your service will still benefit, no matter what your motive. The new mother still enjoys a delicious meal, whether her visiting teachers brought it out of love for the mother or because they wanted recognition.

The new family will still get their furniture unloaded, whether the elders quorum showed up because they have fun together or because the family really needed them. Whatever the motive, the job still gets done. The needy still benefit from the service.

True. None of these motives for service is wrong. None is bad. In fact, learning to serve with the pure love of Christ is a process. None of us serves for the purest of reasons from the moment we begin serving. We all serve for some of these lesser reasons on the path to becoming more Christlike.

These lesser motives, however, are full of potential personal hazards. When we rise above them and our motives for service become pure, we won't feel discouraged or disappointed, exploited, taken advantage of, or unappreciated when serving.

The Personal Hazards of Lesser Motives

How is it that lesser motives may potentially leave the servant feeling exploited, manipulated, unappreciated, disappointed, resentful, taken advantage of, and all kinds of other negative emotions?

Much of the time, when an individual serves with one of the lesser motives, he is counting on mankind to give the reward he seeks. He is depending on a human being to adequately recognize or reward him. When he puts his trust in the arm of flesh, he's bound to get disappointed.

First of all, no human being can fully comprehend the cost of your service to you personally. No human being can understand the pleasures you gave up, how much those pleasures mean to you, or the distress you may have endured during the planning and rendering of the service. They may never appreciate how it terrifies you to speak in front of a group. They may not understand what extreme courage it takes for you call a stranger out of the blue and introduce yourself.

Humans may see your offering on a superficial level, but they don't have clear insight as to what went into your offering. Therefore, when human beings attempt to compliment you, their words may feel shallow or inadequate. And they may well be. It is very difficult for another person to comprehend what went into your labor of love.

When we depend on mankind to give us recognition, we put ourselves in a highly vulnerable position. Chances are, no one will offer any recognition at all, and even if they do, the recognition may seem insufficient. When people put their hearts and souls into their callings and expect adequate recognition but do not receive it, they develop hurt feelings. They may quit their callings and in some cases quit coming to church altogether.

Perhaps you recognize the description of the Primary teacher who accepts a calling and serves in a whirlwind of enthusiasm for six or eight months. She brings tablecloths and decorations, goodies and handouts, crafts and object lessons, activities and birthday presents; she plans home visits and weekend outings. If ever there was a wonderful Primary teacher, she is it. But the children still misbehave in class. She finds her handouts strewn in the hall after church. The students take more than their share of the goodies, and their siblings stop by to sample the treats themselves. The Primary teacher resents the lack of appreciation for her efforts, the lack of respect for her labor of love. At about the nine-month mark, she burns out. Her motives were tainted by a desire for recognition, and when it didn't come, she lost her reason to serve.

This is not to say service doesn't deserve recognition. President Ezra Taft Benson's talk on pride warned us that withholding recognition or appreciation is a sign of pride (see "Beware of Pride," *Ensign,* May 1989, 5). Although each of us definitely has a responsibility to express appreciation to those who serve in the Church, it is dangerous for a servant to become dependent on that recognition as the sole reason for extending the service. The recognition may or may not come, and even if it does, it may or may not feel adequate.

Further danger lies in serving for the recognition of men. Not only does the servant risk receiving no recognition, but he risks receiving criticism.

There is a sign at the ballpark where one of my sons plays baseball: "Never criticize a volunteer unless you want to be one."

Those of you who have observed little league sports can see why such a sign is appropriate. There are always the few moms or dads who yell at the umpire. They yell at the coach. They yell at the players and they yell at the other parents. Just like the "armchair quarterback," these bleacher-front parents think they know how to play baseball better than the current volunteers.

The human tendency to offer one's two cents' worth is so widely recognized that we have coined the phrase "Everybody's a critic." Whether a fair critic, an informed critic, a credible critic, or a dubious critic, people seem to want to voice an opinion—even when nobody asked for that opinion. Criticism is likely to occur, whether it is deserved or not, whether the servant puts tremendous effort into a project or no effort. When a servant's primary motive is the admiration of men, criticism or even lack of adequate praise can devastate his enthusiasm.

I was teaching a Gospel Doctrine class once, and my toddler was not old enough to enter the nursery. My husband was serving in another ward, so he could not watch our son. While I stood at the front of the chapel with a chalkboard and taught the class, my fourteen-month-old entertained himself by crawling up and down the two stairs that led to the stand. On one occasion he discovered the hymnbooks tucked underneath the front pew, and he started taking them out and dropping them on the floor. An elderly woman rose from her seat in the back of the chapel, walked to the front of the chapel, snatched the hymnbooks from the floor and complained, loud enough for the entire class to hear, "I can't believe anyone would let her child do that."

Needless to say, I spent some time licking my wounds. I had to ask myself why I was there teaching and remind myself that it was not for the approval of men, but of God, and I didn't think Heavenly Father was upset with me for doing the best I could under the circumstances. After some serious introspection I mustered the courage to stand up and face the Gospel Doctrine class again.

If we make sure our motives are pure—that we are serving only to bless others' lives—then we won't let the recognition of men be the reward we seek. By doing so, we won't be subject to disappointment, which leads to burnout, which leads to quitting. And, most important, other folks can be blessed by our service in the future, because we will continue to serve with enthusiasm as long as we are able.

THE PURE LOVE OF CHRIST

The last motive Elder Oaks lists is "the highest reason [to serve] of all. In its relationship to service, it is what the scriptures call 'a more excellent way.' (1 Cor. 12:31.)" ("Why Do We Serve?" 15).

The motive to which Elder Oaks refers is charity, or the pure love of Christ. I believe charity is called the pure love of Christ for two reasons. First, because those with charity love as Christ loves; they care so deeply for the individuals they serve that they would lay down their lives if necessary to insure the individual's salvation. Individuals who truly experience charity want nothing more than the salvation of mankind.

"The pure love of Christ" appropriately describes charity for another reason. Those who love Christ keep the commandments of the Savior. They serve because Christ asked them to serve. They feed his sheep because the Savior cares about his sheep. These individuals truly love Christ.

What of the eternal rewards that Elder Oaks claims are also worthy motives for service? An understanding of charity helps us recognize that the eternal rewards might be the very same as charity. What could Heavenly Father possibly give us in the eternities that would be rewarding? Mansions of silver surrounded by streets of gold? Fields of strawberries and forests of redwoods?

Doctrine and Covenants section 18 helps us understand what types of rewards await the obedient in the eternities.

"And how great is his joy in the soul that repenteth!

"Wherefore, you are called to cry repentance unto this people.

"And if it so be that you should labor all your days in crying repentance unto this people, and bring, save it be one soul unto me, how great shall be your joy with him in the kingdom of my Father!

"And now, if your joy will be great with one soul that you have brought unto me into the kingdom of my Father, how great will be your joy if you should bring many souls unto me!" (vv. 13–16).

It sounds as if bringing souls unto Christ, which is a pursuit persons with charity desire more than anything, may be the very same thing as obtaining an eternal reward. The greatest reward we receive in the eternities may be to celebrate with those souls who have come unto Christ!

CHAPTER 18

~

SERVICE FOR
THE FUN OF IT

SERVING WITH THE PURE LOVE OF CHRIST CAN bring the servant greater joy than any secondary motive. Service will become a delight, not a drag, when you purify your motives. Instead of counting the days until your release, you will hope you are never released. Instead of "needing a break," you will find that the service becomes your respite. Rather than experiencing burnout, you will experience invigoration. Heavenly Father wants us to learn to serve out of love because we, the givers, will enjoy the service, as will the recipients.

A stake president came home from the stake center late one Thursday night, bounded into the bedroom, and woke up his wife with an enthusiastic smack on the lips. "You sure have a lot of energy for such a late hour," she mumbled.

"I feel boundless energy," he told his wife. "Working with the Saints invigorates me. I feel like I get more out of working with the Saints than I give."

Wouldn't it feel great if rendering service affected us all that way? I can't help but picture President Gordon B. Hinckley, who at more than ninety years of age serves with the energy of a man half his years. President Hinckley shares the secret to maintaining such vitality and energy: "Why are missionaries happy? Because they lose themselves in the service of others. Why are those who labor in the temples happy? Because their labor of love is in very deed harmonious with the great vicarious work of the Savior of mankind" (*Teachings of Gordon B. Hinckley* [Salt Lake City: Deseret Book, 1997], 595). "Do you want to be happy? Forget yourself and get lost in this great cause" (ibid., 597).

Wouldn't it be nice to feel as enthusiastic about service as the Brethren do? Wouldn't it be nice to have so much energy that you begged for more people on your home teaching or visiting teaching route? Wouldn't it be nice to lie down at night feeling satisfied and energetic rather than overwhelmed and drained?

I believe that every act of service you render can leave you feeling invigorated. However, of all the reasons people serve, the ultimate motive, the pure love of Christ, is the surest way to discover the kind of invigoration the prophet describes.

HITTING THE BULL'S-EYE

Before you jump right in and start serving, you would do well to pause to carefully consider the needs of the people you serve. If you truly want to bless those you serve, you will want to ponder carefully and pray to discern if your act of service will benefit the recipient. You would be shocked at how often good-hearted people think they are helping their fellowman when what they have decided is helpful service really isn't helpful at all.

Once upon a time there was a family whose children were in danger of being removed from the home. The Department of Child and Family Services visited the home and found it so filthy they decided it was not fit for human habitation. They gave the mother two weeks to clean up the home or they were going to take the children and put them in foster homes. When the visiting teachers of the ward discovered the plight of this mother, they zoomed over like a pack of honeybees and cleaned her home. For the first time in years the children could walk down the hall without stepping on clothing. The layers of grime were scraped from the countertops, and the family discovered the color of the Formica.

The problem was, the sister with the dirty house didn't believe in doing dishes. "I don't do dishes," she told her visiting teachers. She insisted that dishes were the responsibility of the children, and if the children didn't do the dishes the dishes didn't get washed. Therefore, when the Department of Child and Family Services came to check the home a few months later, it was in the same state of filth as it had been previously, and the children had to leave the home.

The visiting teachers felt that their service had been for naught. The mother didn't change, and they resented the fact that their tremendous act of service had not yielded the results they had hoped for.

Psychotherapists call these well-intentioned individuals who want to zoom in and rescue the poor and the downtrodden "enablers." Well-intentioned Christians all over are available to rescue the needy. But does it truly bless the needy? These rescuers may at times enable the needy to continue their irresponsible lifestyle simply because they learn someone will always zoom in and bail them out. When you pause before you serve and wait for a prompting, you can better discover what will truly benefit the needy.

I once read a story about a mother who was bedridden for the last few months of her pregnancy. Well-intentioned sisters appeared daily and cleaned her house, dropped off meals, and washed the family's clothes. But all these acts of service made the bedridden mother feel absolutely miserable. She felt helpless, indebted, and worthless. Eventually, a sister visited who had pondered at length the needs of the bedridden mother. She put herself in the mother's slippers and imagined how she would feel in a similar circumstance. Instead of doing the laundry, this sister picked up the baskets of clothes and set them on the bed beside the expectant mother, who could then help fold. She found other ways to help the mother feel useful and contribute in the home. Of all the acts of service performed during the last few months of the mother's pregnancy, this act, performed with a true sensitivity to that mother's needs, brought her the greatest joy.

You can experience charity every time you serve when you truly focus on the person receiving the service. You need only ponder the person's situation, imagine what acts of service will benefit the person, and refrain from the urge to buzz right over and render service to appease your own conscience. Servants who pray and ask for inspiration and guidance can know when the service they render is something that is actually needed. The act of service the recipient truly needs may not be as convenient as the act of service you planned to render. You may not be able to "get it over with" in one concerted effort. However, your act of service will richly bless the person's life because you made sure the service was right on target.

One year at Christmastime my husband and I decided to travel to Utah with our young children. Before we left I had promised my neighbor I would show her how to make gingerbread houses. The day before we left she came over with her seven-year-old triplets (no kidding—two girls and a boy) and we glued gingerbread, dripped frosting, and stuck gumdrops all over my kitchen. By the time we finished we had two delightful gingerbread houses to show for our efforts—and a floor caked with hard, white icing.

She offered to help me clean up, but I assured her it could wait. I needed to spend my afternoon packing because our flight left early the next morning, so we left the site of revelry and my family and I headed to Utah.

While in Utah tragedy struck our family. My grandmother and my aunt were murdered in their mountain cabin. We spent the holidays mourning their deaths and the frightful circumstances surrounding the murders. We delayed our return to Florida so we could attend the double funeral.

Instead of being excited about a fun-filled vacation, and relieved to be home, we returned feeling lost, lonely, and alienated from our loved ones. We retrieved our car from the Park and Fly, loaded our bags, and drove to the brick and mortar structure that awaited us. We didn't feel like we were going home. We felt like strangers, arriving as guests in Florida.

We hefted our bags into the laundry room and flicked on the lights in the kitchen. Suddenly that haunting feeling that we didn't belong in this state vanished. Greeting us was not the frosting-caked floor I had left, but pristine, sparkling linoleum. The kitchen table was piled high with fresh bread, lunchmeats, cheese, and fruit. In the center of the table stood a cake, iced with white frosting, and two words in blue squeezed out of a tube: "Welcome Home."

My sweet neighbor, with whom I had baked gingerbread houses three weeks before, knew exactly how to provide comfort in a time of need. She knew I would be coming home to a house with nothing in the refrigerator and lunches to pack for school. She must have guessed that I'd never have time to scrub that vast floor, and still pack for our trip, and she must have imagined how it would feel to come home to a dirty kitchen. But mostly, she sensed that when we arrived back in Florida we would need comfort, love, and the blessing of knowing folks out here cared about us too and mourned our loss.

Serving with charity as your only motive may entirely change the way you serve. You may rethink tradition and serve in a way you have never served before. Hallelujah! Service is going to become a whole lot more fun.

A BONUS YOU DIDN'T BARGAIN FOR

When you learn to serve strictly to benefit the recipient and not for your own benefit, you will very carefully choose your acts of service, making sure your service truly benefits the recipient. With these stricter criteria, you might find that fewer opportunities for service present themselves. Your service may not be as plentiful as it once was, but it will be more effective, and you will find greater satisfaction in the service. You will feel renewed and invigorated upon serving, and you will not hesitate to serve again. Instead of feeling overwhelmed because so much is demanded of you, you will relish the opportunities to serve that come your way. You might find yourself doing less but enjoying it more, and making a bigger difference.

Once you become more discriminating about the acts of service you perform, you will find yourself saying no to the invitations you feel are inappropriate. As a result, you will have a far shorter "to do" list. This alone will help you feel less overwhelmed.

EXPECTING CHANGE

"But, Sister Smith," you say, "I do serve out of love. I already exercise charity. The needs of others are most assuredly first and foremost on my mind and sometimes I still become discouraged."

Sometimes we honestly serve for the benefit of the recipient but we grow discouraged for another reason. When the recipient of our service doesn't benefit the way we anticipate—they fail to repent, they don't improve their lives, they refuse to embrace the gospel—the reason we experience discouragement is because we expected something from them in return. We expected them to improve their lives. And our expectations are not always met.

We do not spell out our expectations in a contract when we begin our acts of service. We don't warn those we serve, "I'm willing to work my fingers to the bone on your behalf, but you sure better shape up in the end." However, if you pay attention to your thought processes when you begin your labor of love, you may discover that you expect the people you serve to turn their lives around. You might expect them to get baptized if they are not members. If they are less-active members you might expect them to start coming out to church. You might expect wayward youth to repent and serve missions or make covenants in the temple. Although you don't state it at the beginning of your service (either to them or to yourself), deep down inside it's likely you expect to see some results from all your hard work.

Once again, when you expect results from your service you put your trust in the arm of flesh, and that's not a very secure place to place your trust. When you serve with the expectation that others will change, you set yourself up for disappointment. You may work very hard to fellowship investigators who ultimately may not join the Church. You may work very hard as you visit the less active, drop off gifts, make phone calls, and perform other acts of service. And all the while, the less active may remain less active.

You can grow really discouraged and burn out on service if you set your heart upon results. When you keep your part of the unwritten bargain and those you serve repeatedly renege on their part of the unwritten bargain, you may want to give up. The problem here is not so much that the people you serve don't respond. The problem lies in the unwritten contract they don't even know exists. When you expect everybody you serve to respond to your service, you're bound to be disappointed. Like the jilted lover who refuses to ever love again, Saints who serve and have their overtures rejected may give up all hope of effecting change in people's lives.

You will survive your acts of service with far fewer casualties if you serve without strings attached. A gift freely given for the benefit of the recipient doesn't demand anything, not even changes on the part of the recipient.

CHECKING YOUR EXPECTATIONS

Discouragement can be prevented if you refuse to set your heart on people's changing. When you begin your act of service, recognize that the miracle of conversion is truly a miracle. For people to experience the mighty change of heart—that change that leaves them with "no more disposition to do evil, but to do good continually" (Mosiah 5:2)—is like moving a mountain. The statistical chance that every person you chose to serve will respond positively to your service is pretty slim.

In fact, of all the souls that have ever received bodies, not very many will actually become sanctified. In Nephi's vision of the history of mankind, he notes the scarcity of righteous Saints: "And it came to pass that I beheld the church of the Lamb of God, and its numbers were *few*, because of the wickedness and abominations of the whore who sat upon many waters; nevertheless, I beheld that the church of the Lamb, who were the saints of God, were also upon all the face of the earth; and their dominions upon the face of the earth were *small,* because of the wickedness of the great whore whom I saw" (1Nephi 14:12; italics added).

When Bret came home after a series of interviews at the church, I could always tell whether he had been working with people in the throes of sin or whether he had been working with people engaged in repentance. When he had been conducting temple-recommend interviews, he would come home elated, similar to the stake president I mentioned at the beginning of this chapter. He was absolutely on cloud nine after hearing the testimonies of valiant Saints.

However, when he came home discouraged and downtrodden, I knew whoever he had been working with was in the midst of sin and didn't want to repent. His heart ached for the sinner. He agonized about how he could help, and he mourned when he could not. In fact, when asked, "What's the hardest part of serving as a bishop?" Bret didn't focus on the long hours or the late-night phone calls. He responded, "Seeing people mess up their lives."

THE MIRACLE OF CONVERSION

Even when people are lucky enough to be introduced to The Church of Jesus Christ of Latter-day Saints, only a percentage will listen to the missionaries. Of those who take the discussions, only a percentage of these actually join the Church. Of those who get baptized, less than half remain active. Among those active Saints, the ones who live the gospel to its fullest truly stand out from the crowd.

We may not recognize that conversion is a miracle because we see it happen in front of our very eyes. But true conversion, nevertheless, is one of the most miraculous experiences known to man. It can't be explained by science. It can't be manufactured in a laboratory. It comes only with divine intervention. And then only when we contribute a broken heart and a contrite spirit.

Helping our brothers and sisters become converted is somewhat like panning for gold. You leave a lot of stones in the stream for every good nugget you keep. We learn in the book of Helaman the rarity of true conversion: "And I would that all men might be saved. But we read that in the great and last day there are some who shall be cast out, yea, who shall be cast off from the presence of the Lord" (Helaman 12:25).

Nevertheless, the difficulty of the work and the rarity of finding real gold doesn't stop people from panning for gold. Likewise, we still send missionaries into all the world, even to the countries that do not baptize large numbers of people. Each elder spends two full years on his mission, even if he doesn't baptize one person the entire time he's gone. Just because we are not guaranteed results does not keep us from trying.

We have been instructed repeatedly by the Brethren that when fellowshipping nonmembers, we need to make sure we remain their friends, even if they choose not to take the discussions or to join the Church. For example, Elder M. Russell Ballard counseled: "I encourage you to build personal, meaningful relationships with your nonmember friends and acquaintances. . . . If they are not interested in the gospel, we should show unconditional love through acts of service and kindness, and never imply that we see an acquaintance only as a potential convert" ("The Hand of Fellowship," *Ensign*, November 1988, 30).

Naturally, we hope that our labor will bear fruit. We hope that the individuals we serve will taste the delicious fruit of the gospel of Jesus Christ. But we must remember that every soul on earth has his or her agency, and some may not use their agency to seek salvation.

We may serve with all our hearts, and the individual we serve may still choose not to repent and choose not to live the gospel. We might serve with all our hearts, and the person's repentance progresses so slowly that we grow weary with the waiting. One bishop, recognizing the discouragement of leaders who do not see progress in those they teach, tries to encourage his quorum leaders, "We're responsible for the effort, not the result."

Remember Moroni chapter 9: "Let us labor diligently; for if we should cease to labor, we should be brought under condemnation" (v. 6). My husband learned this principle after some desperate soul-searching as a young missionary in Argentina. The missionaries had been instructed to "obey all the mission rules with precision so miracles can happen for you and your companion." Several months went by, and Bret kept the rules to a tee. (This is a man who had not missed attending a single general priesthood meeting from the time he became a deacon until he left on his mission.)

After several months of perfect obedience, young Elder Smith expected this miracle he had been promised, and he was certain this miracle would manifest itself in the baptism of a well-beloved family he and his companion were teaching. However, this particular family rejected the challenge to be baptized and stopped taking the discussions.

A discouraged and disheartened Elder Smith sat at Sister Motto's kitchen table with his head in his hands and wept. "What more could we do? We have done everything the president asked, and this family still won't be baptized." His tears dropped in puddles onto the butcher block.

Sister Motto, an elderly Lamanite with creases in her cheeks and white streaked through her hair, sat in front of the distraught elder and stuffed tissues into his hand. "Elder Esmit," she said ("Smith" sounded like "es-smeet" when she spoke his name), "these people have their agency. It is your job to teach them the gospel. It is their job to accept it."

BE THE AUDIENCE

Service can take on a new meaning if you approach acts of service with a new attitude. Try to begin your service with a sense of not knowing what will happen. If you do, you may well experience the wonder and amazement of a spectator. Instead of playing the role of a director, manipulating the performance of those you serve, allow them to surprise you. Should they put forth some effort and begin to change their lives, you will be pleasantly surprised. Should they refuse to embrace the gift you offer them, you need not grow disappointed. You were only an observer anyway. They are the actors in this play. The script they chose to follow simply did not have a happy ending. Some don't.

RESPONSIBLE FOR THE EFFORT

One more hint may make it easier for a servant to avoid focusing on results: recognize that you are blessing others' lives simply by giving them the opportunity to hear the gospel.

Everybody needs an opportunity to hear the gospel, and everybody needs the opportunity to repent. You would be doing others a disservice to deny them this opportunity simply because they didn't appear to be likely candidates for sainthood.

A twenty-something young man did not fit the mold of a "golden contact." This beach bum was seriously addicted to alcohol, had had his driver's license revoked for too many DUIs, spent his sober moments surfing, and did not have an education or a viable job when the missionaries taught him the gospel. Yet he devoured the truth like a starving child. He read the Book of Mormon over and over again. He read everything he could find on modern-day prophets and temples and eventually joined the Church. He returned to school and found gainful employment. He accepted a very responsible calling in the Church. He married a lovely young Latter-day Saint woman in the temple, and they began a family. The missionaries had to exercise considerable faith when they began teaching this alcoholic and feckless young man, but they put forth effort, and he produced results.

This story could have ended differently, with the same set of missionaries putting forth the same amount of effort. Ultimately it is the decision of every individual who walks this earth whether or not to embrace the gospel of Jesus Christ. When we cross paths with one who does want to change, and we witness the miracle of conversion firsthand, we should thank the Lord for our good fortune at having been an instrument in his hands to teach the one with the heart of gold. Ultimately it is that individual's good heart responding to the Spirit that caused the change, not our exceptional effort.

If the service you render doesn't bear immediate fruit, you can further assure that you avoid discouragement when you remember the beauty of agency. Were it guaranteed that the people you serve would repent, neither of you would experience any joy in their decision. Their decision would be "par for the course," "old hat," "boring," "no surprise." If everyone repented and everyone were forced to repent, there would be no victory in overcoming the evil one.

Perhaps that's one of the reasons the Lord promises us that our joy will be so great when we bring but one soul unto him (see D&C 18:15). It is the greatest victory in life to overcome the evil one. The miracle of conversion is no less a miracle than that of birth. Should you labor all your days and bring save it be one soul unto Christ, you will never look at that one soul without remembering all the stones you left in the stream. You can better understand the tremendous worth of a soul when you consider to what lengths we go to bring souls unto Christ.

CHAPTER 19

ENJOY THE RIDE

SERVICE IN THE KINGDOM CAN BE A WILD RIDE. It's likely that you will chug your way to the top of one challenge, and for one split second feel like you've arrived, just before another surprise launches your stomach up into your throat. You will get tossed and thrown from side to side, all the while clutching tighter to the hand of your dearly beloved companion. And when life calms down for a moment and you coast your way to stillness, you'll look at one another and exclaim, "That was fun! Let's go again!"

Supporting a spouse who is steeped in Church service means that both of you will serve. You will serve right alongside your spouse as you both care about the same flock and together go out to visit and nurture individual sheep. You will serve together in the same great cause, your beloved attending to his or her stewardship while you attend to yours. You will serve your sweetheart by lifting emotional burdens that come with demanding callings. You will serve your sweetheart as you lift physical burdens that he or she is prevented from attending to, in light of a demanding calling.

Service inevitably causes the servant to develop feelings of brotherly love for those served. Your sweetheart will develop feelings of love for the individuals he or she serves—compassion for the Saints of Zion. Your spouse will learn patience, and faith, and hope. During the course of service, your spouse will develop charity—the pure love of Christ.

And so will you.

You will develop compassion for those you serve. You will learn patience and faith and hope. During the course of your service you will begin to feel the pure love of Christ for those you serve. And who have you served most faithfully? For whom have you patiently listened to complex feelings, reassured when overwhelmed, offered suggestions when asked, bailed out when overcommitted? For whom have you served with everything you have to offer? For this one you feel love greater than any you could have felt without such service.

This blessing, a stronger marriage and deeper affection for one another, is a blessing you experience because you both have accepted a call to serve. Serving together in the kingdom can bring as much joy to your union as you two bring to the lives of those you serve. By serving together and supporting one another and bearing one another's burdens, you will develop love beyond measure for the individual who rides by your side and who will serve by your side throughout eternity, your dearly beloved companion.

INDEX